Dawoud Bey

on Photographing People and Communities

Introduction
by Brian Ulrich

aperture

Table of Contents

Introduction

By Brian Ulrich

I first became aware of Dawoud Bey's profound work when I went to the opening of his exhibition, *Portraits 1975–1995*, at the Cleveland Center for Contemporary Art. At the time, I was more interested in experimental photography so I don't quite recall how I ended up at the opening. His pictures were a far cry from the work I was responding to by photographers like Larry Clark and Nan Goldin, but I was instantly struck by the lush detail of Dawoud's large Polaroid prints; they confounded me. After some time weaving through the crowd and examining the work closely—from afar and then close again—I learned my first lesson from Dawoud. I became aware that the people attending the opening, mostly Northeast Ohio elites, were vastly different from the people in the portraits, and I realized that Dawoud planned to create this dynamic, bringing the underrepresented onto the walls of the museum to spark critical dialogue. This was as much a part of the work as the photographs themselves. He intended the encounter with the pictures to show the common humanity between different communities, changing the ideas that the attendees might have had about those in the portraits. I understood the interaction between the photograph and the viewer completely differently after that exhibition.

A few years later, I decided to pursue a graduate degree in photography. I wrestled with the question of whether I had something to contribute to the field through my own work and told myself that two to three years of study would provide the answer. I chose Columbia College in Chicago to be part of the city itself, its community of photographers, and of course because of the faculty, where Dawoud was essential.

In our first year, Dawoud challenged us, his students, in a way that was direct but also empathetic. In an early critique, I put up photographs taken on the streets of Chicago, part of a not-yet-fully-formed idea for a project. Dawoud spoke at length about others who had defined this genre, pointing to only a few recent photographers who had reinvented what is possible in photographing strangers in public. I took his frankness as a challenge, telling myself it was worth further exploration. As a teacher, he made us aware of the obstacles ahead of our work in a way that helped us to see and respond to the difficulties of contributing something new in a medium long trafficked by others before us.

In my last year of graduate school, I took a class with Dawoud simply titled, "The Portrait." He passionately explained his belief that something inherently powerful can happen between a sitter's psychological state and the resulting mirage that is the photograph. To this day, I am in awe of the moment a portrait is made, of how one can render an identity into an image. In that class, Dawoud also gave sage practical advice, encouraging us to build upon successes: "Always start with your last best picture." He taught that intuition might produce a profound photograph and that we needed to lean into those images rather than labor over things that didn't work. This advice applies to more than just photography.

Though Dawoud was always interested in why and how we, as photographers, did what we did, he was equally invested in our ability to sustain a practice, guiding us in how we might achieve our goals. He explained that the steps to a successful career were a matter of making opportunities for ourselves: "If the work is good, and the photographer is taking steps to get it in front of an audience, something is bound to happen." His reassurance that efforts would yield results—for both the work and its reception—fueled our ambitions.

When visiting artists came to speak with students, Dawoud always asked them candid and probing questions about the practicalities of a creative life—support, finances, successes, and failures on their career path—which gave us a glimpse of what our futures might look like, and more important, the steps we might take to arrive there. He often reminded us that if we were truly committed to our practice, we were "signing up for a lifetime." Studying with Dawoud not only formed my deep understanding of the photographic medium—an understanding which always informs my work—but also gave me the confidence to pursue a career as an artist and a teacher, continuing in his tradition of sharing that knowledge.

Outside the classroom, there were countless hours of advice and conversation over lunches, coffees, and break-fasts where we discussed making work in relationship to the broader happenings in culture, or the role of an educator in this contemporary climate. Other times, he would invite people to his home to play music (getting to play bass to Theaster Gates's drums was a highlight). In short, Dawoud is welcoming and generous; and he is purposeful in forming communities of support and friendship between those who are interested in making and speaking to our culture, in changing and affecting the world with both small and grand gestures. This carries over from his work, which continues to recalibrate our understanding of the world and point to the potential in us all.

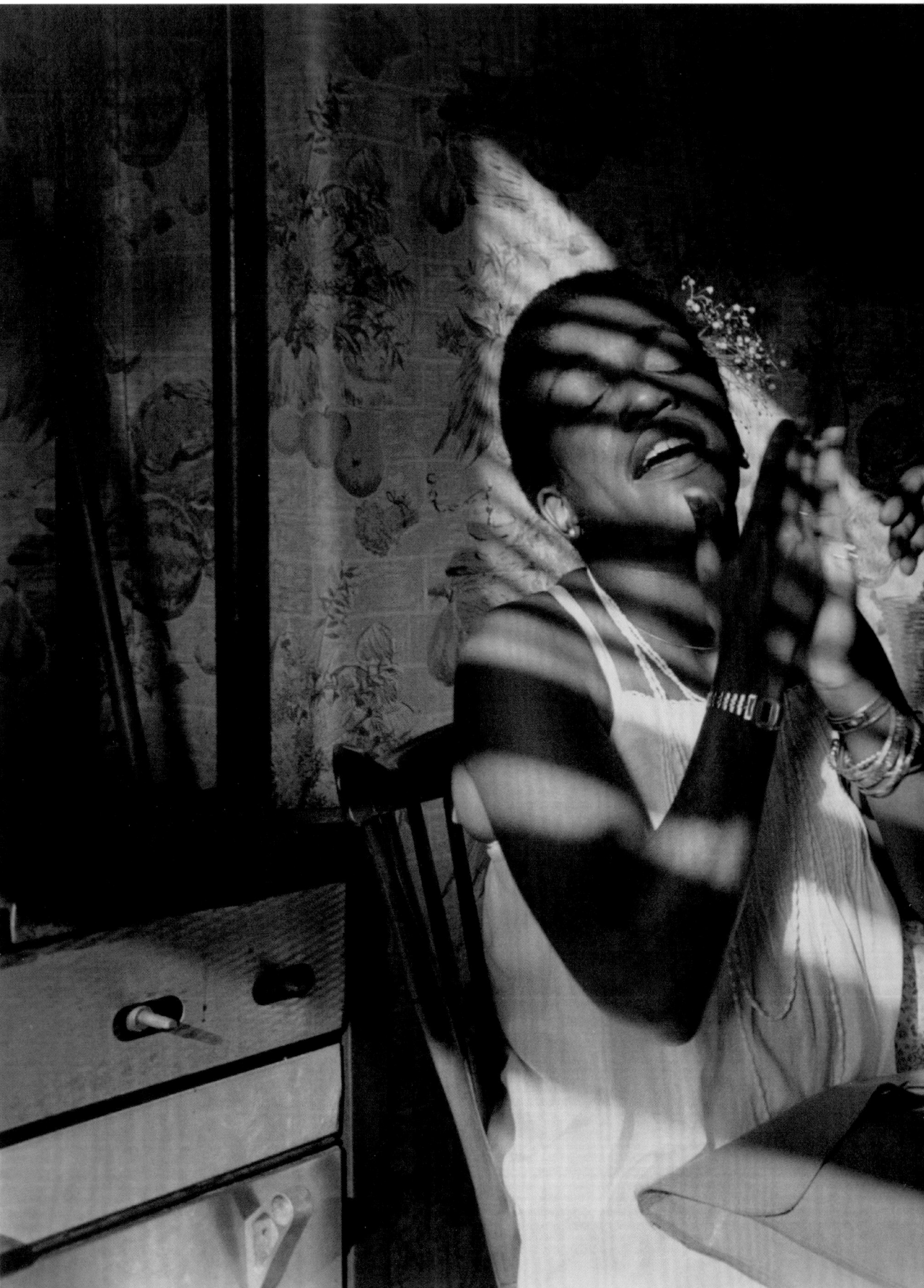

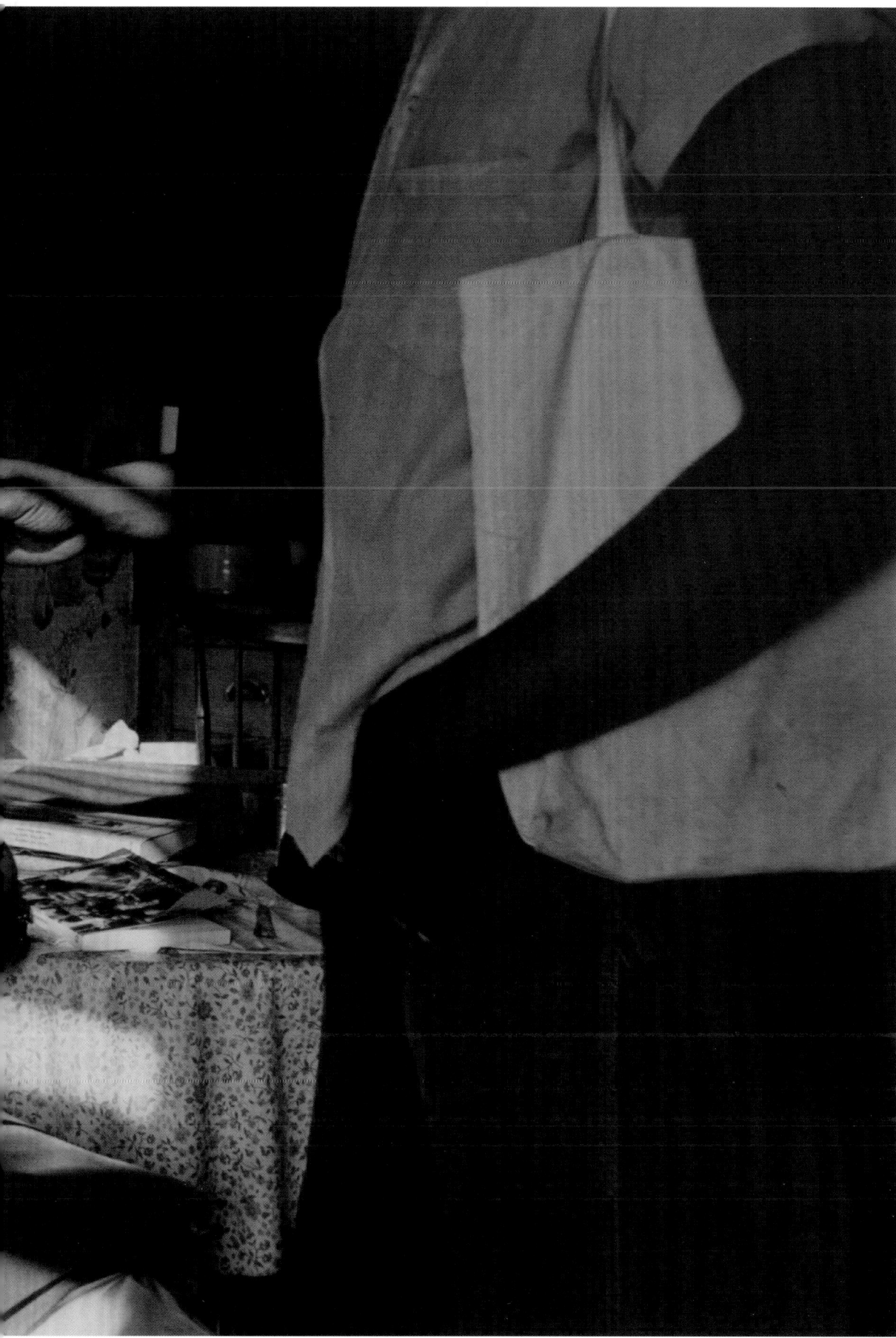

People in Front of the Camera

Making art always involves being able to manifest an idea, in photography's case making it visible. You use the camera to transform what you see into a new experience, anticipating the image you wish to make but also being open to chance or external elements that could transform the image and your expectations.

My ideas have largely centered on the human subject; I'm interested in visualizing the human community in a broad range of contexts. The strategy and context may change, but it's always a person or people sitting or standing in front of the camera. Pictures of people in front of a camera—that describes everything that I've done for forty years, every single picture.

My real interest in photography began at fifteen years old. As we were leaving my godmother's house after my godfather's funeral, she said, "Oh, wait a minute. I have something I want to give you. This camera belonged to your godfather, and I want you to have it." Getting that camera, for no reason that was apparent to me, sparked my imagination. I decided I needed to figure out how to use it. I took a class at the Y and started buying photography books and magazines to educate myself about what one does with all the numbers on the lens and the side of the camera. It turns out that as you change the shutter speed from 1/30th to 1/250th, the shutter opens and closes either quicker or slower. That's how I started.

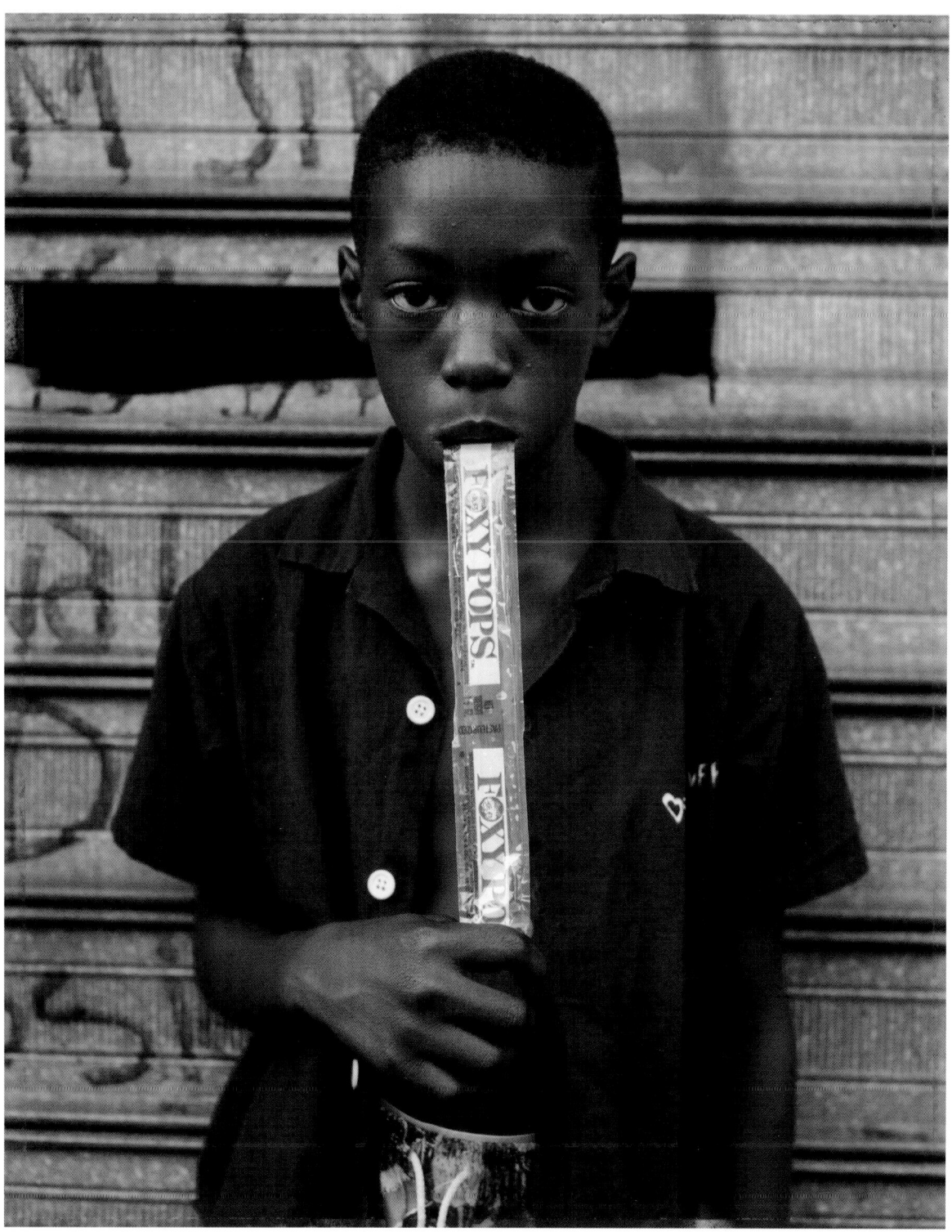

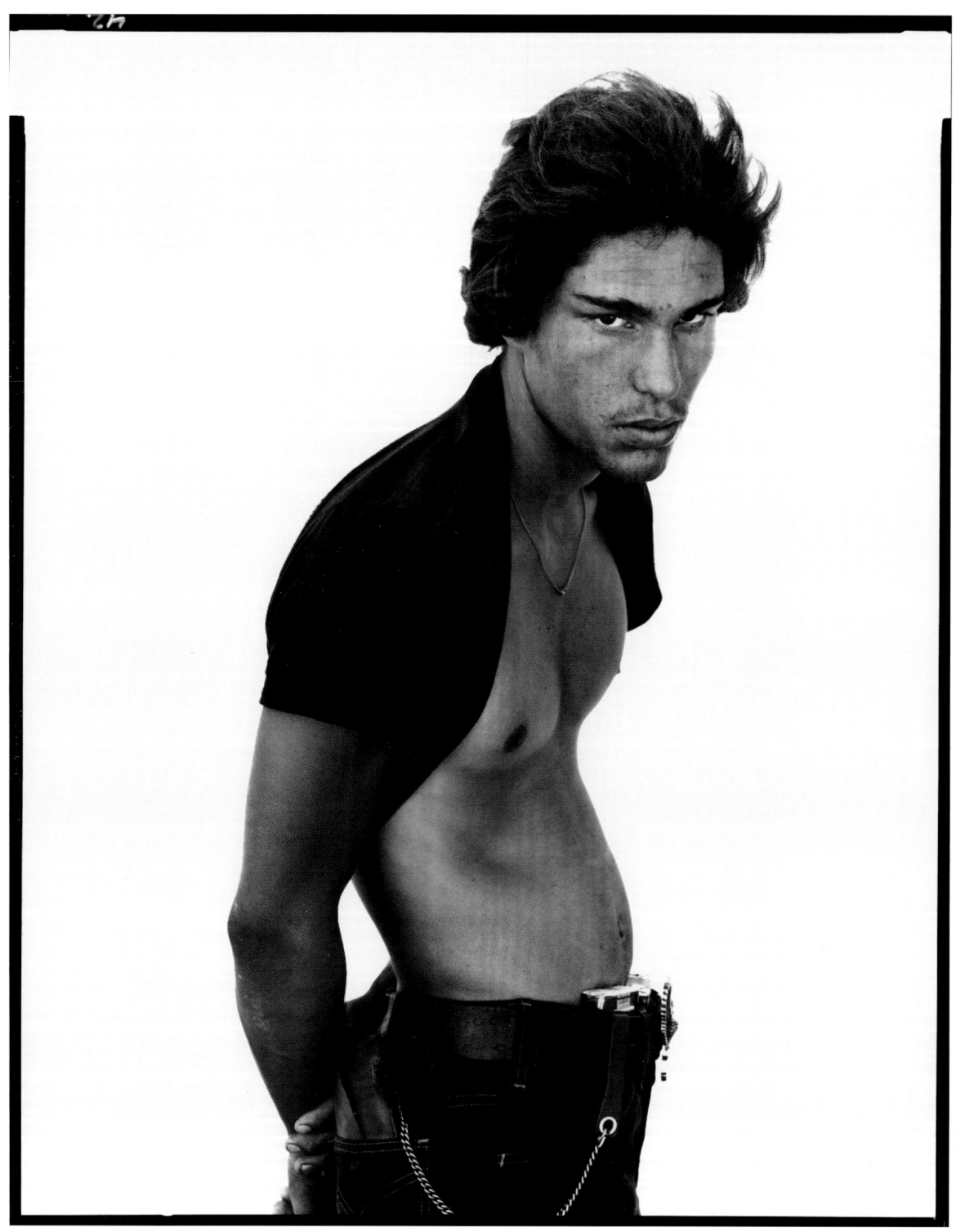

Richard Avedon
Juan Patricio Lobato, Carney,
Rocky Ford, Colorado, August 23, 1980

What Makes It Worthy

I had no formal training at that point. Going out and constantly engaging with photographs was my initial education.

I took it upon myself to look at photographs on the walls of museums and galleries—presuming that if it's on a wall then somebody decided the work should be looked at. If that's true, then what is it about *this* work that makes it worthy?

My dad bought the *New York Times* every Sunday, and the back page of the Arts section had a listing of all the exhibitions. At that time, it fit on one page and, all the way at the bottom, were maybe two or three listings for photography (or sometimes just one). This is how I heard about Richard Avedon's work. The listing was for Marlborough Gallery on West 57th Street. Being from New York, I thought, "I can find that." It was a matter of deciding if I was interested and then putting myself there. I have to tell you though, to provide some context, that going to these museums and galleries on my own was pretty intimidating. There was no one in my neighborhood I could ask: "Hey Tyrone, want to go to 57th Street and check out Richard Avedon?" So, this was a solitary process for me.

Once I got there, I was blown away by Avedon's portraits. Avedon once said, ". . . you can't get at the thing itself, the real nature of the sitter, by stripping away the surface. The surface is all you've got. You can only get beyond the surface by working with the surface." It was clear from seeing his photographs that the surface contains rich information and could provoke a strong response. I was struck by how the portraits convey a credible sense of identity as the person is isolated in the blank, white background. To me, this is what makes a photograph of a person, a portrait.

As I looked at a lot of work, I began to take notice of what interested me. I wanted to make something of my own that resonated as much as those pictures did. I wanted to make something as compelling. That became my challenge.

On another trip to Marlborough Gallery, I saw Irving Penn's *Small Trades*, where he brought ordinary people into the studio in their working clothes, the clothes of their trade. In doing so, Penn gives this black chestnut vendor a heightened sense of importance.

The people in Penn's photographs seem very much at home with themselves despite being in what is clearly a foreign space, which suggests that Penn had a very gentle hand in directing. You have to direct in the studio—the cart has been placed at that angle—but the vendor still feels like he's trying to sell hot chestnuts. He doesn't look like he's been kidnapped from the streets and tossed into the studio, which is what you'd expect his initial reaction to be when Penn asked him to bring the cart with him. There he is in a fancy studio looking like it's the most normal thing in the world, like he belongs there.

The way Avedon and Penn gave everyday people this level of attention became something I wanted to emulate. I thought that was profound—that you could move folks out of their surroundings and into the context of the studio. It seemed like a rather simple idea: a person in front of a camera can result in something deeply moving.

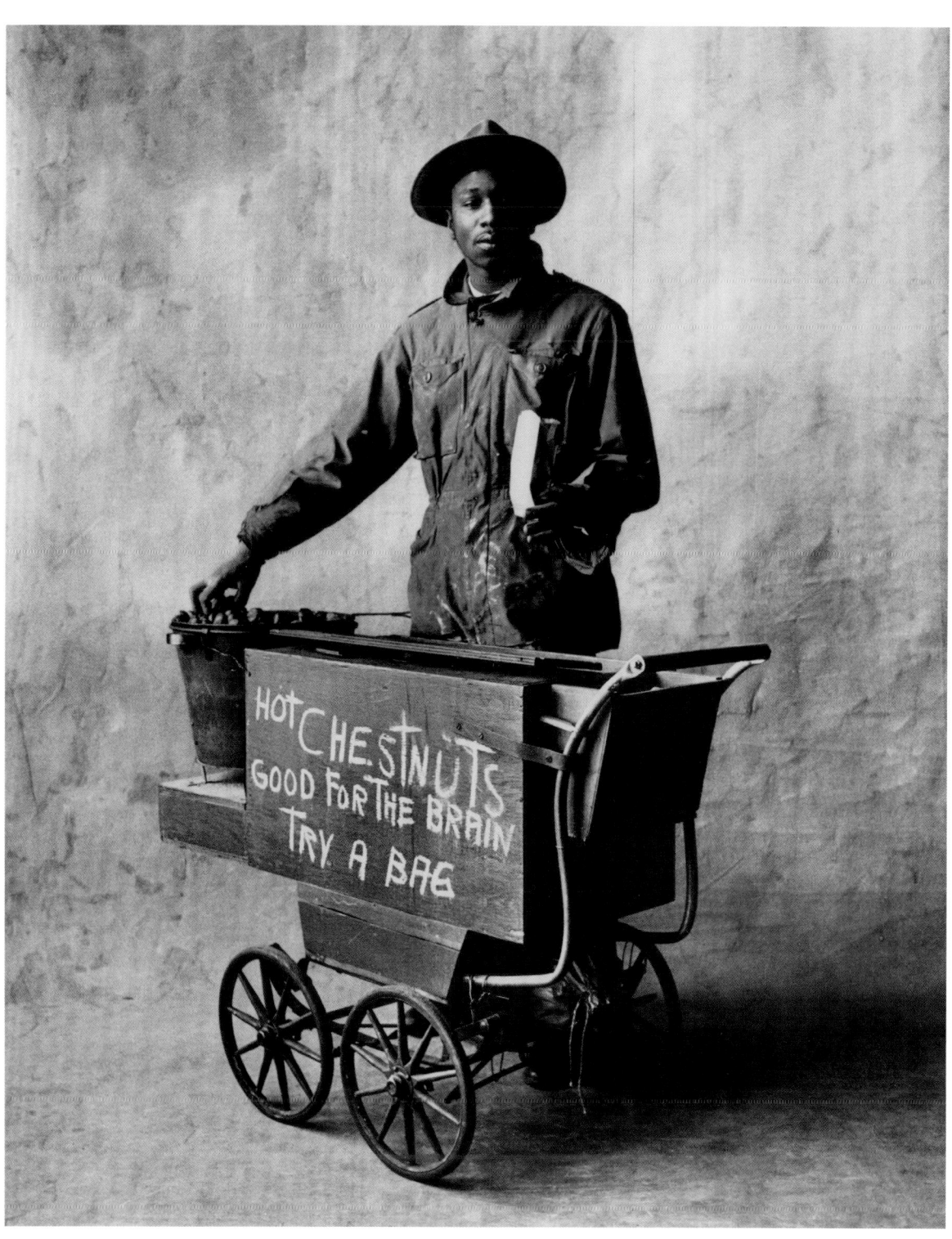

Irving Penn
Chestnut Vendor,
New York, 1951

My first trip to a museum was to the Metropolitan Museum of Art to see the *Harlem on My Mind* show in 1969. A lot of controversy surrounded the show, and people were protesting outside. Harlem then was a largely African American neighborhood, and the Harlem community had little, if any, participation in shaping the exhibition. The question of who was allowed to publicly author the experience of a community became a flashpoint. Should the experience of people in the community be authored by those outside the community?

The late '60s and early '70s were a time of speaking back to powerful institutions of all kinds. Being introduced to the museum at that moment, I came to understand it as a charged space that one could challenge.

When I saw the show, I was mesmerized—pictures of black folks, room after room, and other people walking around looking at those pictures. I felt like I had stumbled into a world I knew nothing about. The exhibition gave me a sense of photography's documentary power, its potential to be a repository of collective memory, a doorway into another experience.

James Van Der Zee, who had a studio in Harlem during the 1920s, '30s, and '40s, was one of the few African American photographers whose work was included in *Harlem on My Mind*, and his pictures made the strongest impression on me. They were privately commissioned portraits and only became public through their inclusion in the exhibition. The African American community was portrayed differently in those photographs than the way black subjects were depicted in the public arena of that era, which was usually much more stereotypical and certainly not affirming. The wonderfully elegant sense of formality and classical posing in this photograph lends an air of both dignity and composure to the family portrait.

For Van Der Zee, the subjects came to him as a matter of course. If you lived in that neighborhood and wanted a portrait, you went to Van Der Zee's studio, which is very different than how Penn and Avedon were working, going out looking for people and asking them to come to the studio. I realized that a portrait results in one of two ways: the subjects either seek out or are invited in by the photographer. This may not be evident in the photographs, but how they came into being and who they're made for has meaning.

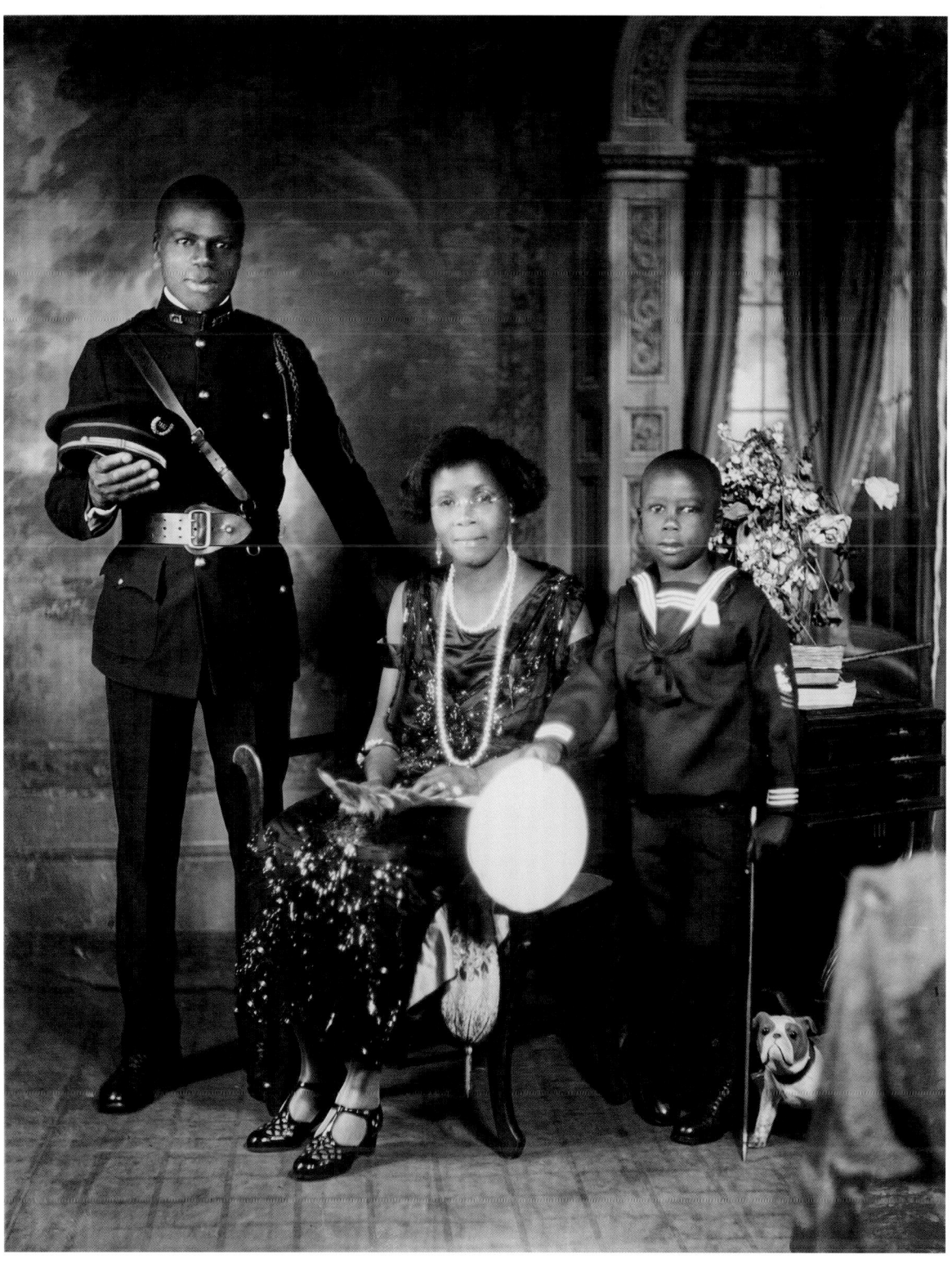

James Van Der Zee
Garveyite Family, 1924

THE SWEET FLYPAPER OF LIFE

Roy DeCarava and Langston Hughes

When the bicycle of the Lord bearing His messenger with a telegram for Sister Mary Bradley saying "Come home" arrived at 113 West 134th Street, New York City, Sister Bradley said, "Boy, take that wire right on back to St. Peter because I am not prepared to go. I might be a little sick, but as yet I ain't no ways tired." And she would not even sign for the message —since she had read it first, while claiming she could not find

(continued on page 3)

Roy DeCarava
Cover of *The Sweet
Flypaper of Life*, 1955

The Long Table

I was moved by the Harlem photographs of Roy DeCarava in a book called *The Sweet Flypaper of Life* (1955), which he published in collaboration with Langston Hughes, who wrote the text. DeCarava was the first African American photographer I encountered who was not a studio photographer making work for people who came in from the streets to be photographed. But he wasn't a photojournalist either, like Gordon Parks, who had made photographs of Harlem on assignment for *LIFE* magazine. DeCarava's pictures were entirely self-motivated; he brought his own subjective vision to bear. He took the African American experience as he knew it, and then wrapped his dynamic aesthetics around the subject matter, which placed the pictures in dialogue both with African American culture and the history of photography.

All of the photographs I was looking at began to shape what I wanted my own subject matter to be. In 1975, I began photographing in Harlem. Certainly, Harlem occupied a large place in black sociocultural production, going back to Langston Hughes, the Harlem Renaissance, Marcus Garvey, James Baldwin, Roy DeCarava, and of course the *Harlem on My Mind* exhibition. Also, though I'm from Queens, my mother and father had lived in Harlem for a number of years. Harlem was both a place in my imagination and also a very real place in my family history. I wanted to make photographs that contributed to the long conversation about Harlem in visual culture.

If you're serious about learning your art form, it's important to learn about the history of the subject you want to speak to. Because, in making your work, you're always engaged in a historical conversation. There's a long table full of people who have done significant things, and then you come along and there's an empty seat. But you gotta have something to say. You don't want to repeat what's been said and you also don't want to say something completely out of sync with the conversation. You have to share a language even if you don't share an intention.

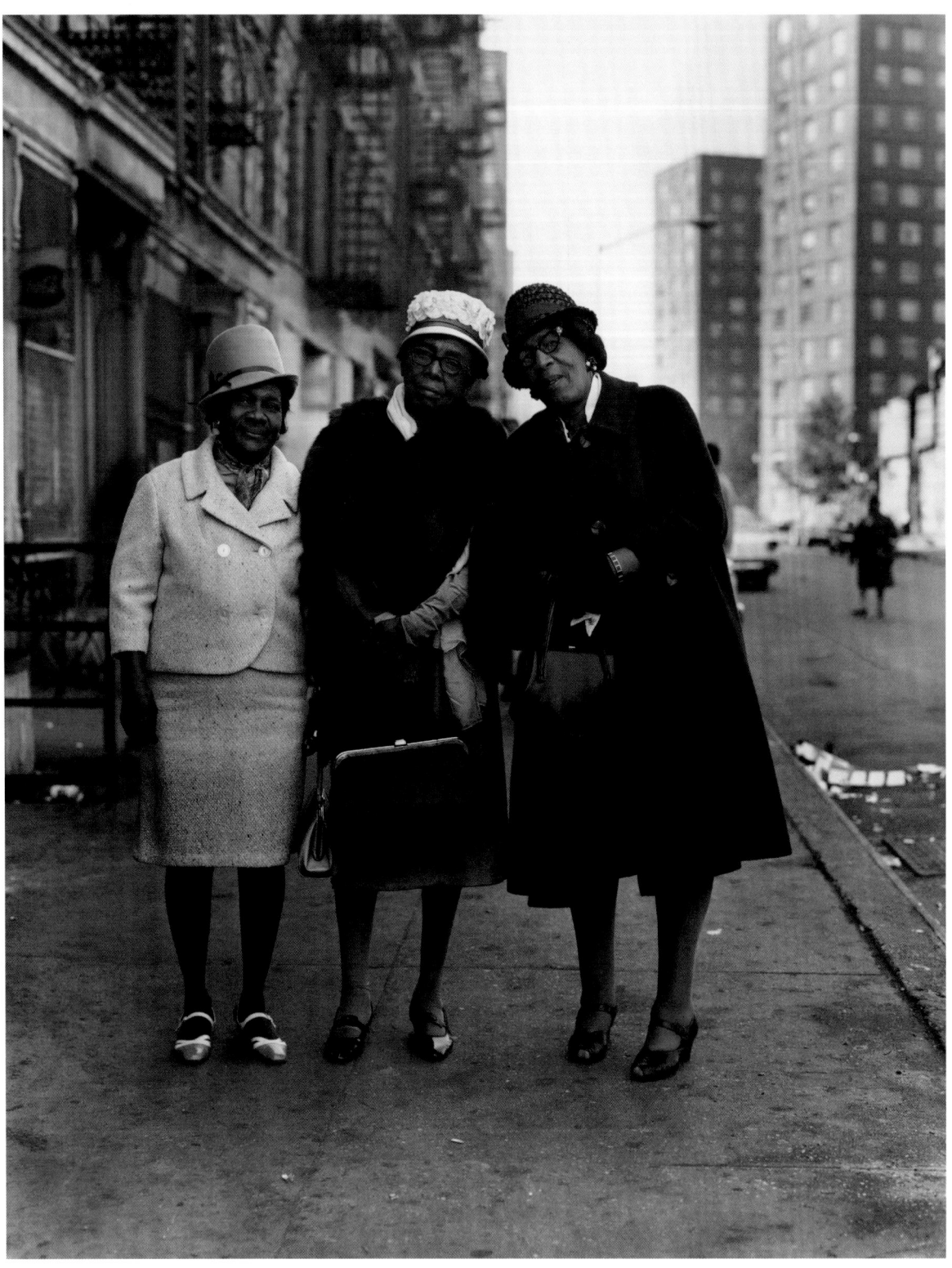

Bruce Davidson
East 100th Street
(Ladies of East Harlem), 1966

22

Transcending Difference

Bruce Davidson was an outsider photographing Harlem with his project *East 100th Street* and some people found that problematic. Aaron Siskind was also an outsider in Harlem. The fact that they were white and not from the community made them double-outsiders. While I may have been African American like the people in Harlem, I was still an outsider. I was a photographer from Queens attempting to represent their community. This question of outsiderness weighed on my mind. How do you create something that empathetically cuts through that outsiderness so that subjects are viewed as more than "look how different they are from me, the photographer, and you, the viewer." What I didn't want to do was create a group of pictures that rendered the people of Harlem as exoticized or pathologized.

I have very consciously taken on issues of presumed difference (age, race, gender) as one of the inherent challenges of all of my work. I try to address questions like, is it possible to transcend the boundaries of difference and make a meaningful representation of a subject? Does one have to be twenty-five years old and black to speak credibly to the experience of someone who is twenty-five and black? Does one have to be gay and white in order to speak legitimately about that experience? Is it possible to make work with some common denominator that transcends lines of difference?

Even when you're a part of the community you're photographing, you may not be able to see it clearly and end up making something overly sentimental. No matter your position, inside or outside, it's a question of intention. There also has to be critical thought applied to that intention. One needs to critique one's own motivation. Not all intentions can be justified. I'm not saying don't make any photographs, but there has to be a moment when you step back and ask what does this photograph mean outside of what makes for an "interesting picture."

I feel Davidson successfully negotiated the matter of difference in this photograph. You can tell by the relaxed disposition of the women. He's not standing outside looking in. They don't look like props in their own lives or props for an idea either. When I'm photographing, I'm careful not to press my hand too heavily or obviously on the situation. Even though I'm shaping the image from behind the camera, I'm also allowing the subject to be themselves.

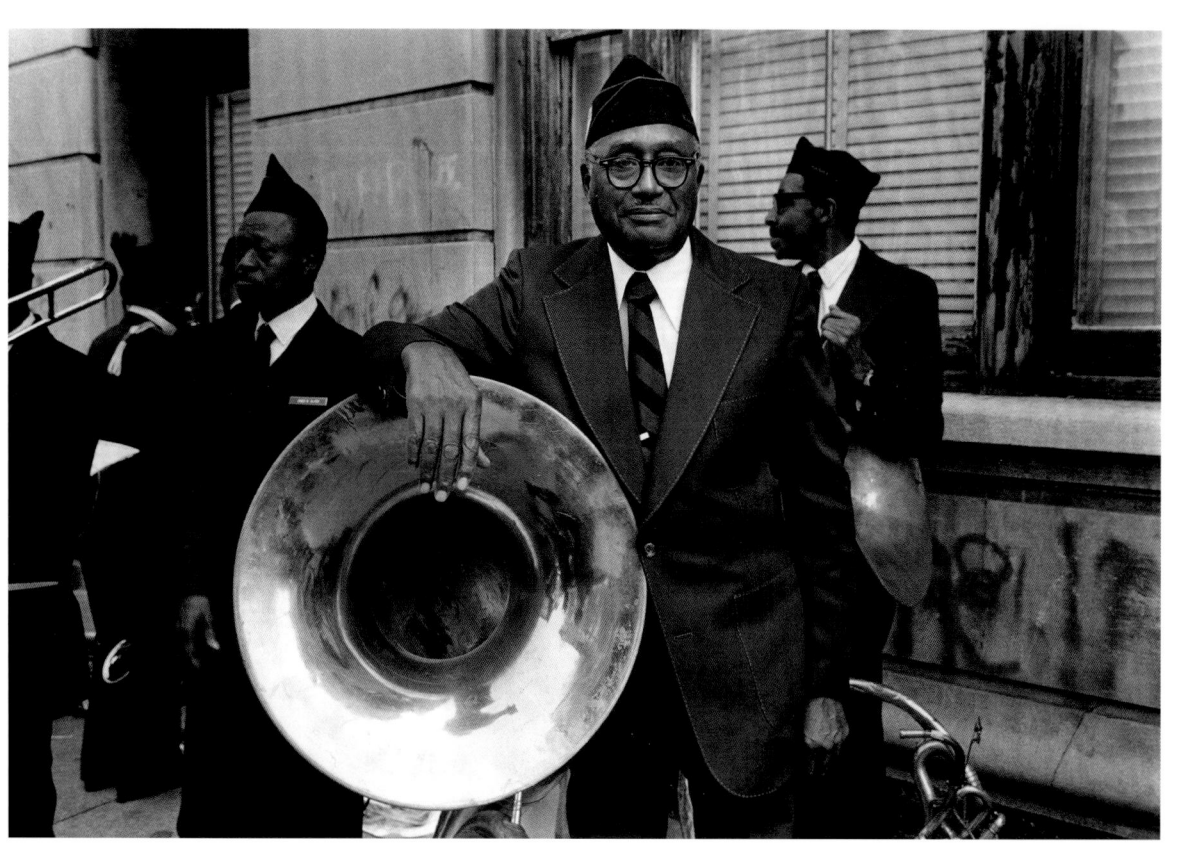

Dawoud Bey
Men from the 369th Regiment Marching Band,
Harlem, 1977

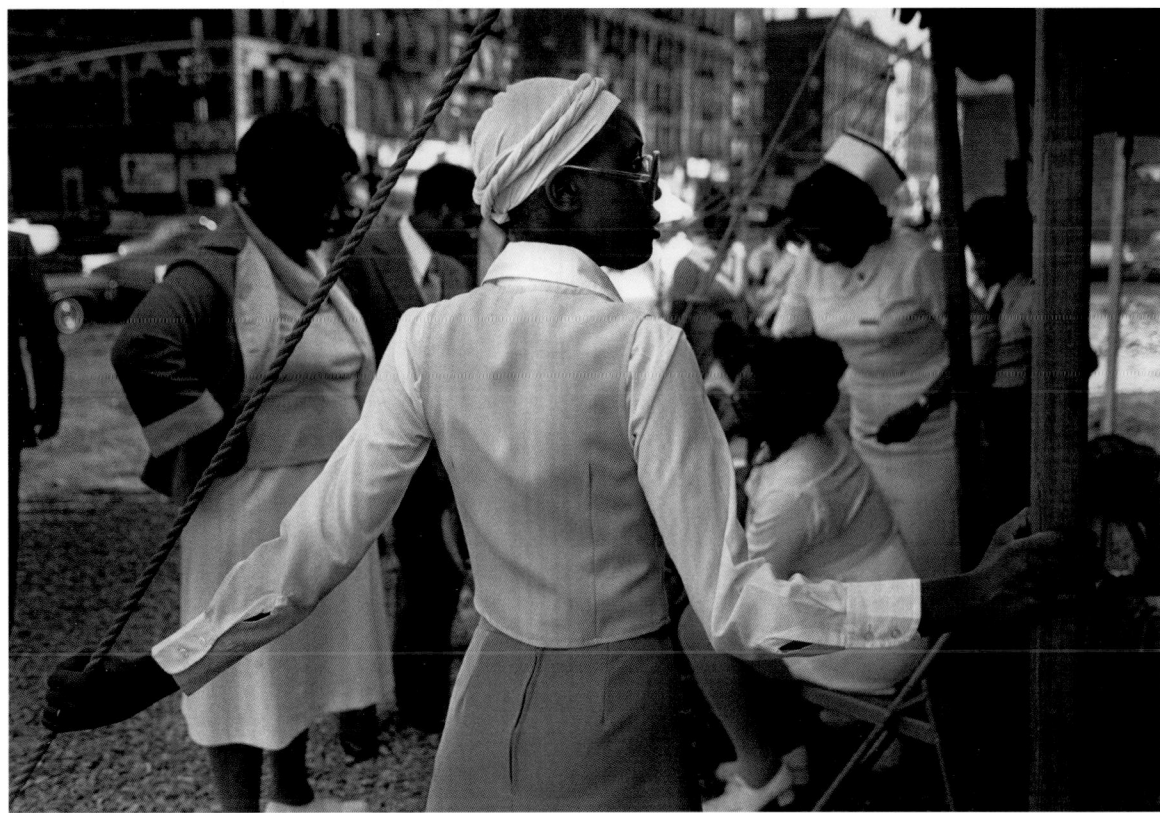

I also immerse myself in the community before I begin photographing. I knew that I had to establish a degree of familiarity with Harlem first, as well as spend enough time walking around in the neighborhood for people to become familiar with me. Once my presence in the community was established, I moved more freely. It was also important to build my own informed relationship with the place because I wanted the photographs to speak to my own sense of Harlem. I wanted to be clear about my own viewpoint.

Though you need to understand where you are and have respect for people, this doesn't mean that you have to move into the community to photograph it. While Walker Evans and James Agee were working on *Let Us Now Praise Famous Men* (1941), Agee was insistent that he needed to live with the people to get the information he needed. He wanted Evans to stay there with him and work too. But Walker was like, "Not me, Man. I'm going to stay in the hotel in town. I'll see you in the morning." The point here is that you don't have to live a subject's life to make something meaningful. You have to know enough to show up and see as deeply and clearly as you can once you're there. You also have to be clear about why you're there. Why are you in this community? How does your subjective viewpoint connect with the actual subject? What is it that you want to say about them? What is it that they might want to say about themselves? How can you bring those two things together in some way through your picture making?

Approaching Strangers

It's one thing to go up to Harlem wanting to make photographs. You're there with the camera, now what are you going to do? Just being there doesn't answer the question.

I wanted to photograph this man in the bowler hat who was talking to a group of three friends and I had no idea how to interrupt their conversation in order to do so. This is when I first realized that it wasn't just about the photograph; it was also about establishing a relationship out of which comes the photograph.

It was extremely difficult for me at that time to walk up to a stranger and say, "Excuse me. I want to make a picture. No, not of all three of you. Only him." As I approached them, I lost my nerve. I just nodded hello and kept walking. I walked all the way to the corner, kicking myself the whole way. I went through a whole psychological head trip: "He saw me once. What's he going to think when I go back again? What's he going to say?"

But I realized that if I was going to do what I said I wanted to do, if I was going to be who I said I wanted to be, I had to approach him. I had to break through my hesitancy about photographing strangers if I was going to make photographs of people. It wasn't going to happen any other way. It helps to push through that uncomfortable feeling if you've thought about why you want to take a picture in the first place, because they're going to ask and you need to be able to say something: "I think you look interesting" or "I like the way you look standing there."

When he agreed, I realized I had another challenge to deal with. I had broken through the social situation, but now I had to figure out the picture-making situation. Once you have the consent, then there's the photograph—the thing you still have to make. How to point a camera at him and come away with a picture that's not just a record but something more evocative?

Where you stand in relation to the subject is just as important as where the subject is standing. I'm always looking at the spatial geometry and the interlocking shapes of the background, then thinking about how to place the figure in the frame. He's right where he needs to be, so I stood slightly to his right to place him in the open space of the frame, so his head wouldn't butt up against the line of the window, and so I could use the environment—the draped window, the railing, and the building itself—to give dynamic form to the picture. And it just so happened that he leaned on the railing and cupped his left hand, bringing the "grace notes" that complete the photograph by revealing something unique to him. If I were making this now, I might have had the camera a little more level to straighten the window up. Formal considerations, like the relationship of the figure to the space, are what make the picture as much as the psychology or the quality of the engagement. But all of those things have to come together so the narrative of the space and the narrative of the individual interact.

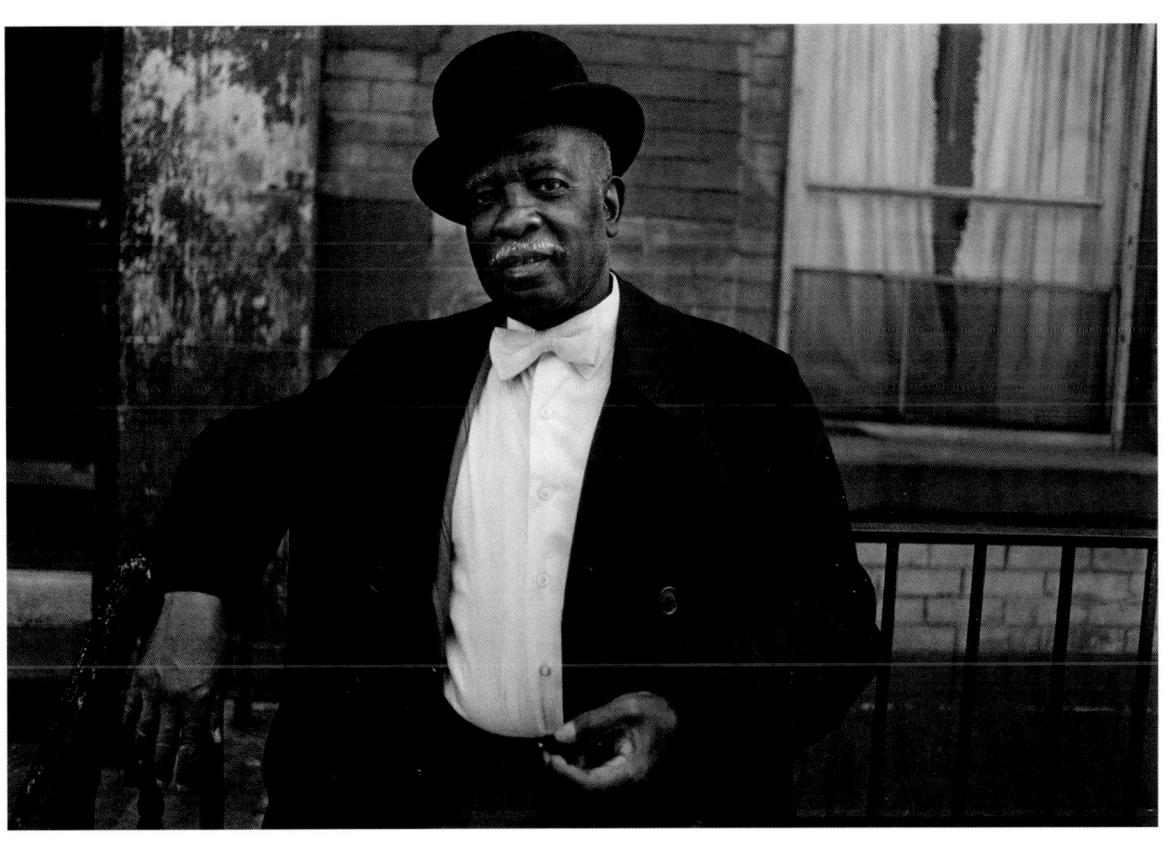

Dawoud Bey
A Man in a Bowler Hat,
Harlem, 1976

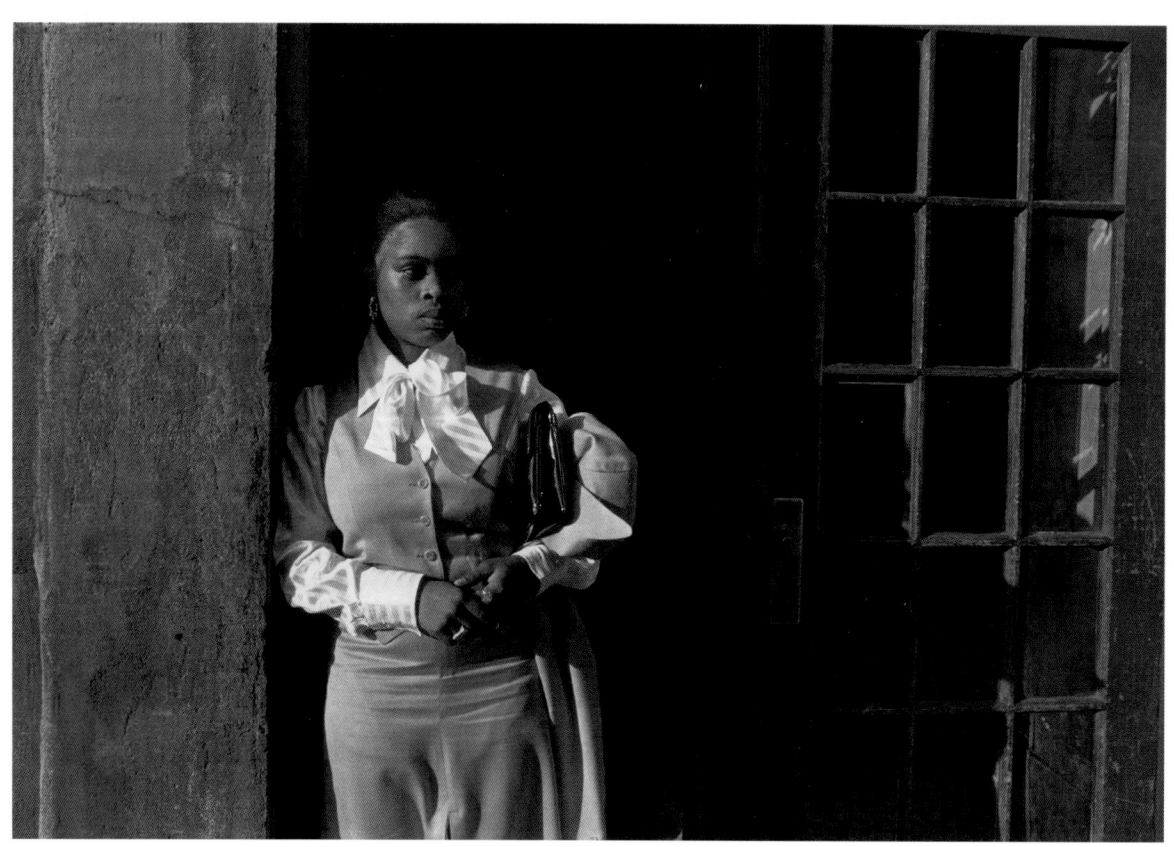

Dawoud Bey
*A Woman Waiting in
the Doorway, Harlem,* 1976

I've never worked with a long lens. All of these pictures are made with a 35 mm camera and a slightly wide lens, which demands that you get close to subjects and have real interactions with them.

Early on a Sunday morning I saw this young woman standing in the light across the street and I wanted to make a photograph. I crossed the street and, as soon as I asked if I could take her picture, she put her arms down and everything changed.

She said, "Sure. What do you want me to do?" While I was thinking about it, a light bulb went off in my head because I wanted her to do exactly what she was doing when I first saw her. So, It dawned on me to just ask her, "Why don't you do what you were doing before I walked up?" Directing the behavior of the person in front of the camera was a huge conceptual leap for me. Before this point, I thought you weren't supposed to interfere with the scene because it compromised the authenticity of the photograph by adding an element of untruth.

This experience gave me the reassurance that ultimately what mattered was not the truth of the scene, as much as what you ended up with in the photograph. It's not the truth; it's a photograph. There's the life of the subject in the photograph, and then there's the life of the subject in the real world. They're related, but they're not the same thing.

From that point on, I became most interested in *describing* the subjects through photographs, not worrying about whether I had directed them or not. I discourage my students from talking about photographing as "shooting" or "capturing" or "taking," because it's really about trying to figure out a way to describe with the camera, to *make* something.

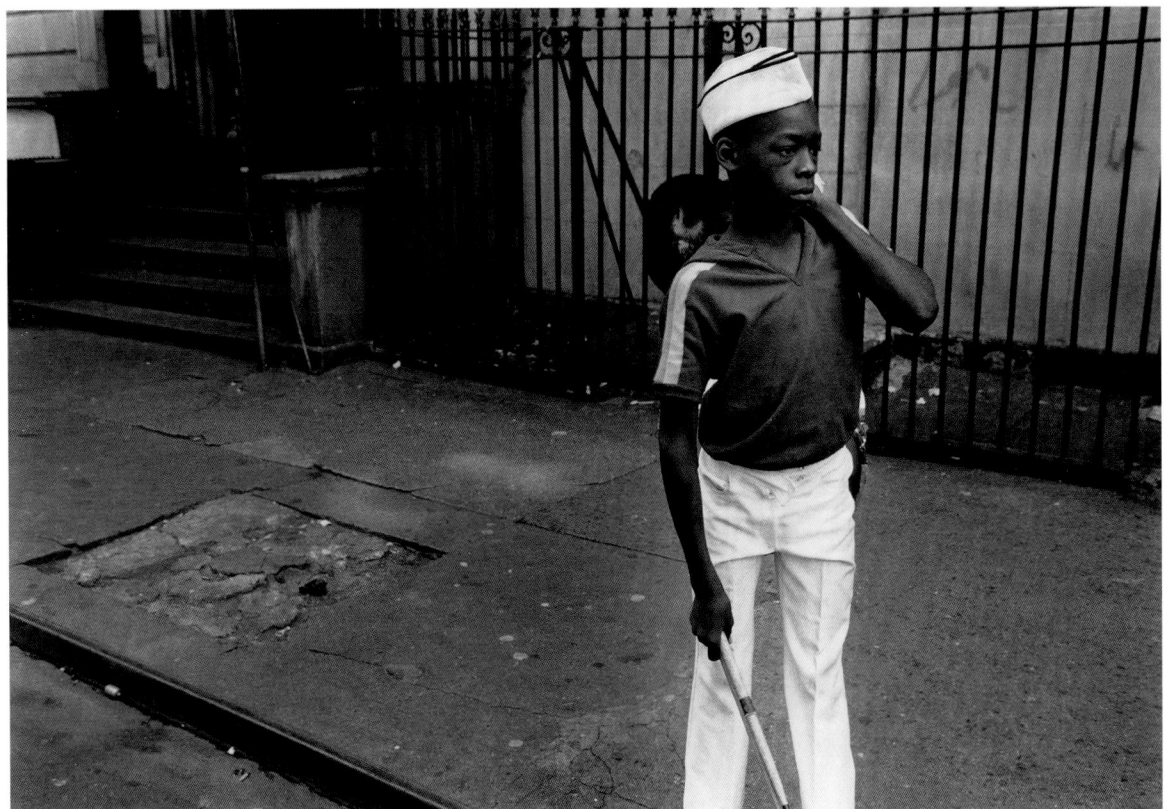

Ten Thousand Hours

My initial creative outlet was actually writing and then music. I played music for a number of years as a drummer. My first sense of what it meant to be an artist came out of that. In his interviews, John Coltrane talked about how he was always practicing, even in the dressing room between sets. I came to know that kind of rigor early on and to understand that you have to continuously practice an art form in order to both achieve and sustain (and transcend) your skill level.

In his book *Outliers*, Malcolm Gladwell theorizes that successful people—across a wide range of fields—have to put in ten thousand hours of practice to reach their level of success. Like any other profession, being an artist requires physically getting up and "going to work." Photographing in Harlem every day was my practice.

The fact that photography only requires a photographer and a camera for its execution really appealed to me. Unlike music, which you have to play with someone else and where you have to wait for people to show up, I could take my camera and go out into the world and make some work. I didn't have to wait for anybody. I didn't have to talk to anybody. I could just go do it.

Dawoud Bey
*A Young Boy from a Marching Band,
Harlem, 1977*

30

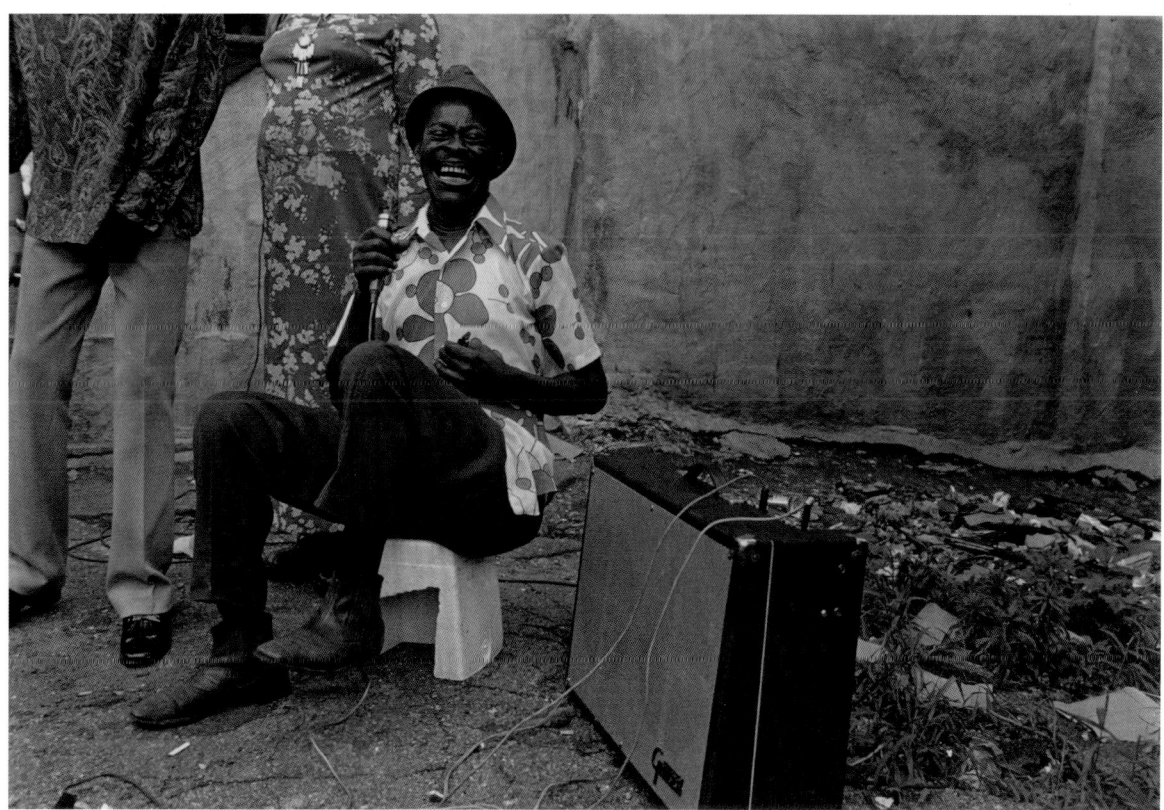

As I went to Harlem more, the resulting photographs became more successful in terms of the goals I had set for myself. These were the first pictures where I was actually doing the thing I had, up to that point, only imagined myself doing.

I had a sense that Harlem was a neighborhood in transition and I wanted to make pictures where the past and the present overlapped with each other in this moment of its evolution. These early successes led me to consider the relationship between artistic intent and making something that lives up to the level of that intent. Once I began responding to my own photographs as strongly as I had to those by other people, I began to feel like, "Hmm, maybe this is something I can do."

Dawoud Bey
The Blues Singer,
Harlem, 1976

More to the Picture

He is stylin' big time. He's cool with his grape drink, his aviator sunglasses, his track-suit, and his white sneakers. We met on the same patch of sidewalk momentarily. I was going that way, and he was coming this way. I thought the movie theater box office with the lights behind him would be as good a place as any to make a photo-graph. I just asked him to stand there, lean on the barricade, and relax. Beyond his style, what makes this picture interesting is that even though he looks very cool and at ease, he's on his tiptoes. He's so young, he's got to stretch to reach the top of the police barricade. He's not quite tall enough but he's acting like he is.

There's more to this picture than a subject who is interesting to look at. I'm always trying for a certain level of psychological depth and perception, for pictures that reward looking closely. This young boy gave me even more than I could have imagined in the moment.

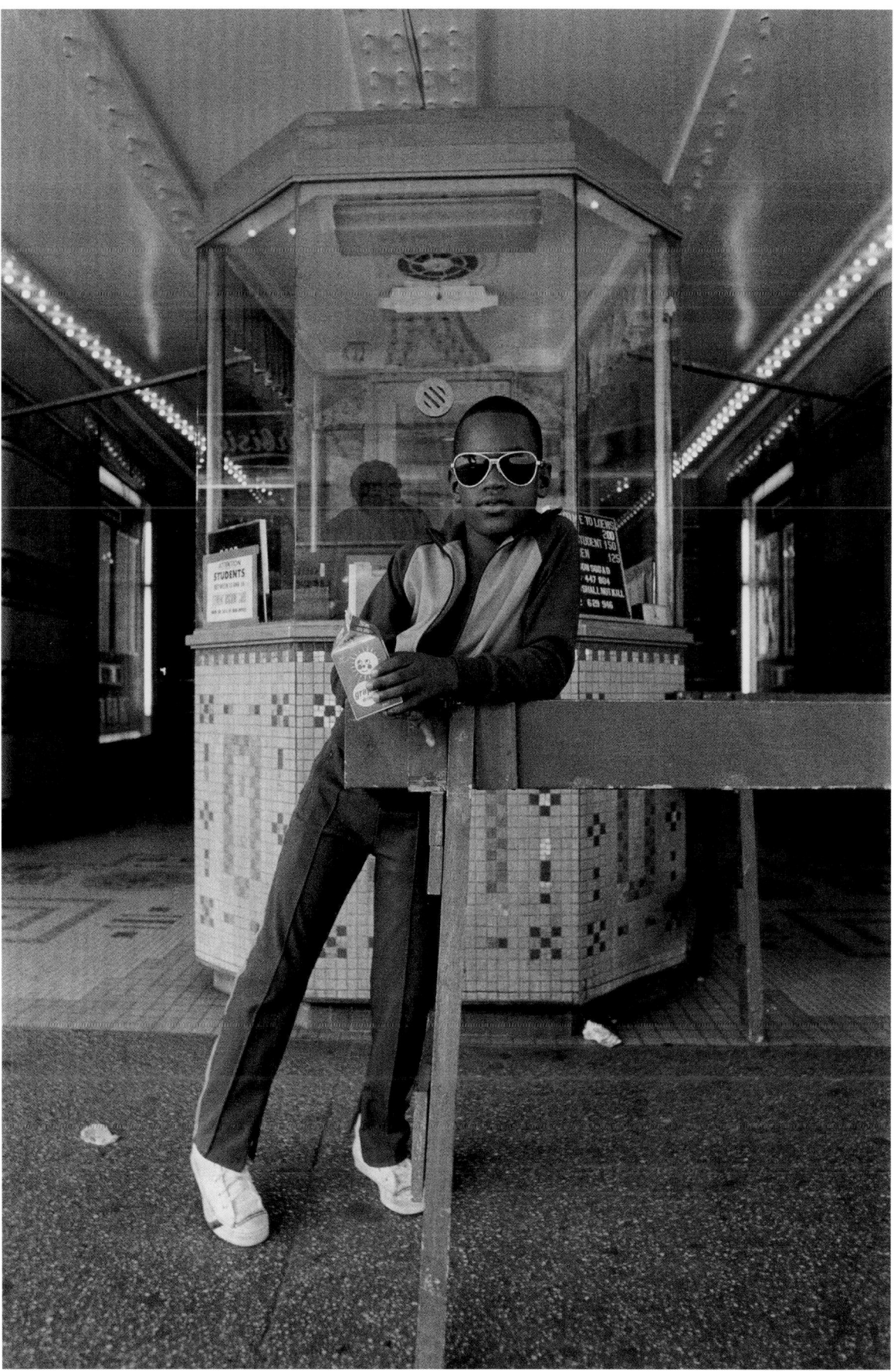

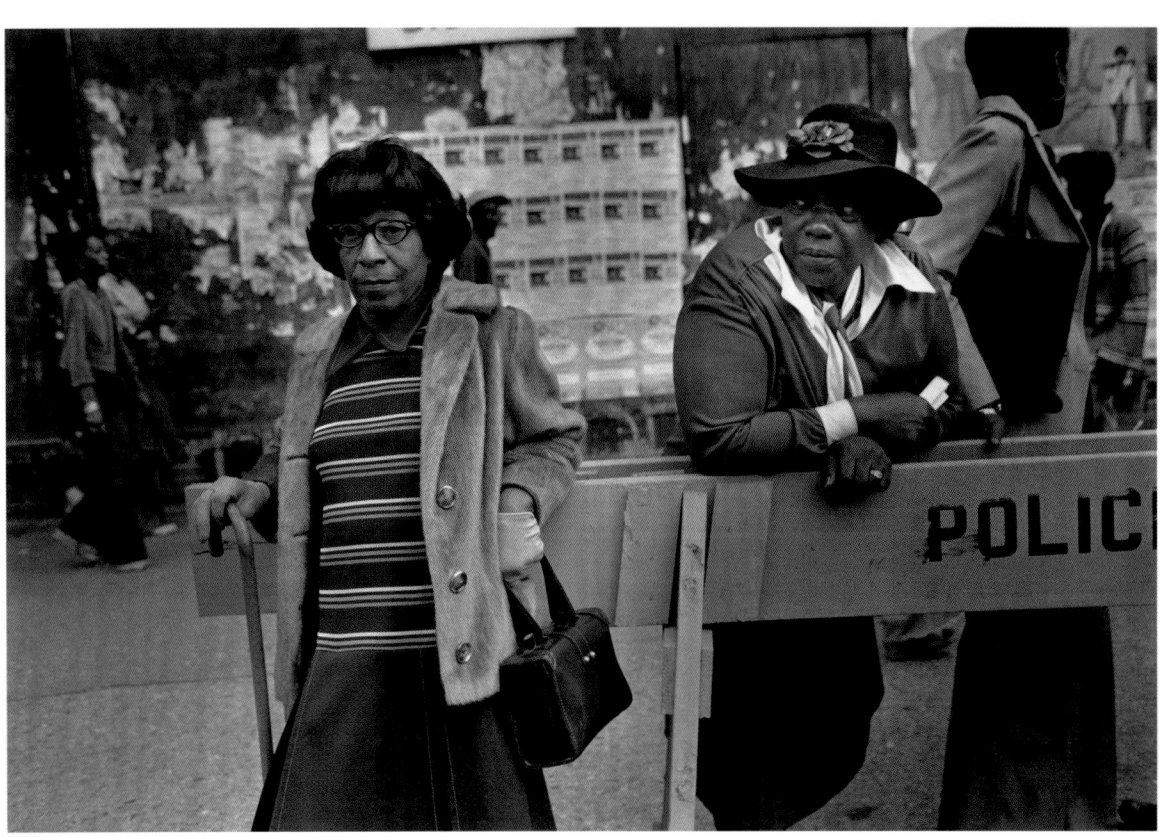

Dawoud Bey
Two Women at a Parade,
New York, 1978

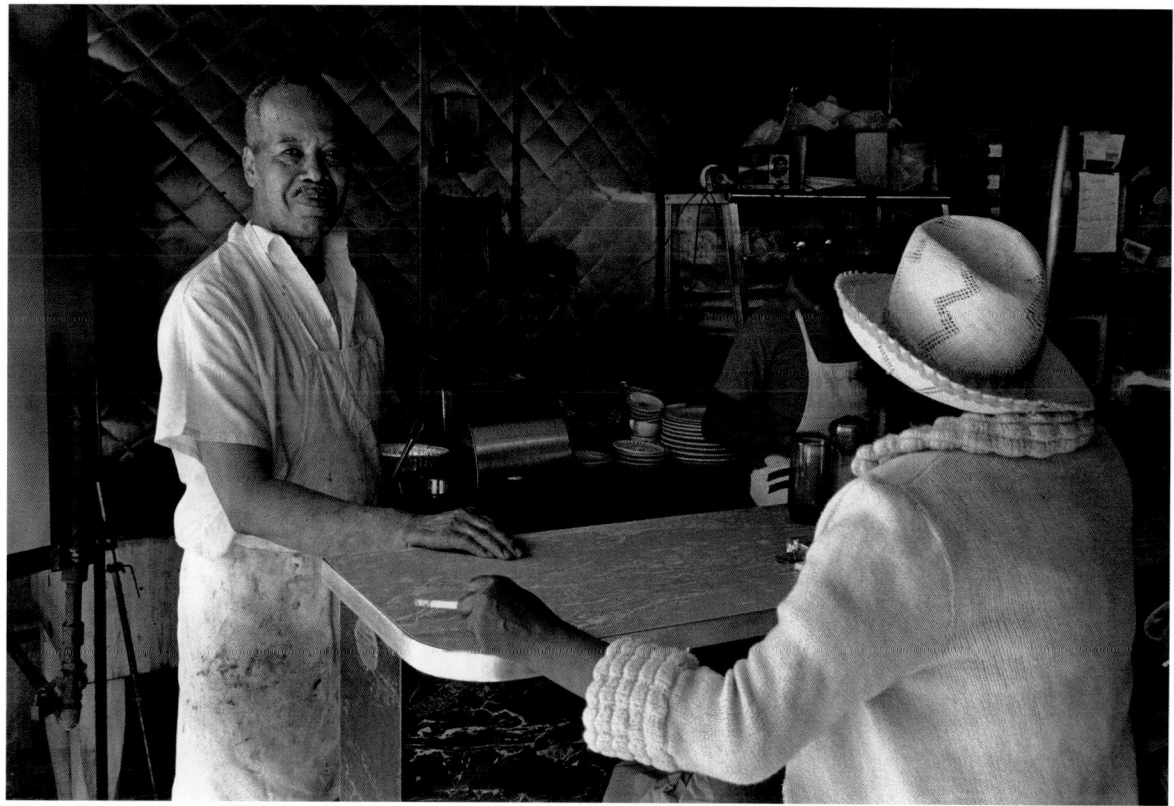

Behind the Camera

Photographing people can easily intimidate them. I'm aware of that and consciously work to make sure it's not a nerve-racking experience; I keep it very conversational. Even though I'm doing a lot of thinking formally and visually about shaping the picture, it just seems like a casual exchange. "Hi, how ya doing? Mind if I take a picture? . . . I'm just out here in the neighborhood making photographs." While I'm asking, I'm putting my camera up to my eye, so the conversation and the picture-making kind of become one and the same. I try not to let the seriousness of what I'm doing, in terms of making a coherent visual description of the person, enter into the conversation. I try to give the subjects their space, while on this side behind the camera there are all sorts of other things going on. They don't need to know what those things are; they simply need to be comfortable enough to be themselves in front of the camera.

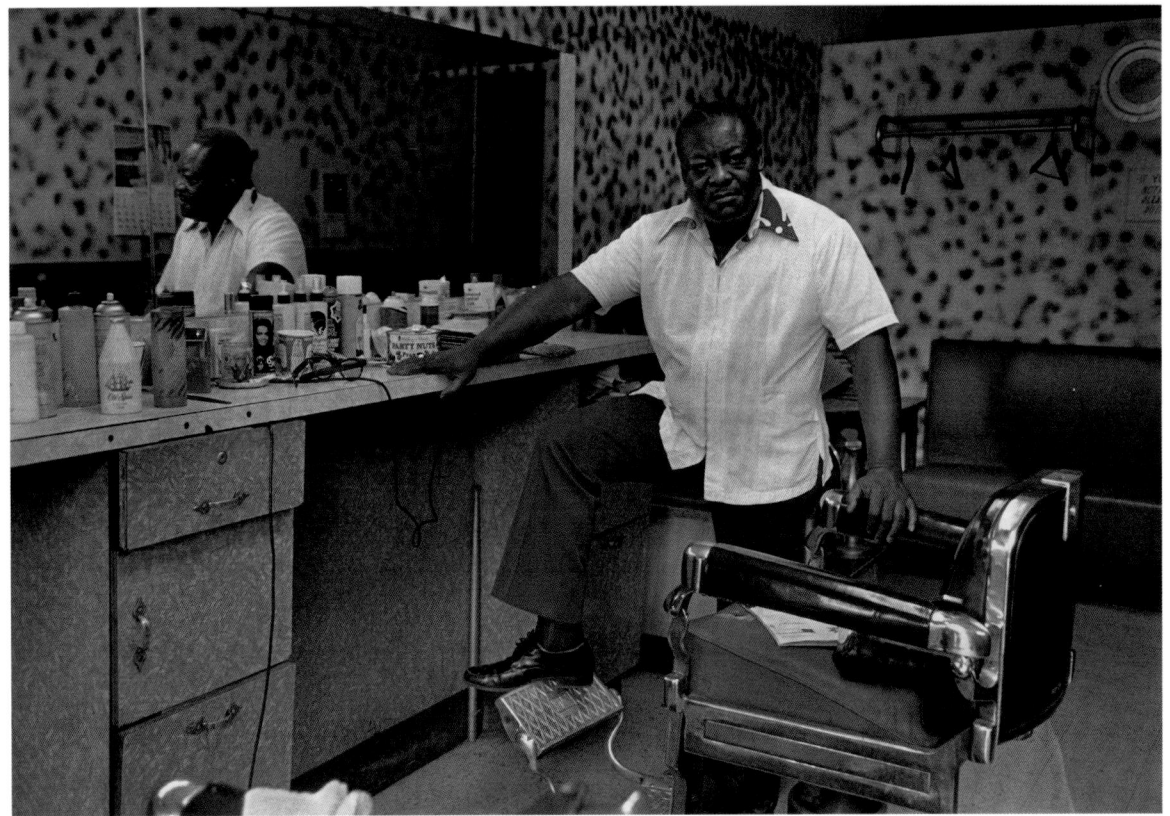

When people are in their environment in a photo, there's a physical connection between the subject and the space that reveals a level of familiarity and comfort.

In making these photographs, I was inserting myself temporarily into other people's lives, careful that the evidence and the breadth of their living was not completely disrupted by my stepping into their space with a camera.

This is a picture of Deas McNeil, who had a barbershop on 7th Avenue between 137th and 138th streets in Harlem. I spent a lot of time in the area around that barbershop and one day I went in when he was alone and asked if he would mind if I made a photograph of him. And he said, "I've been photographed before. When the military was integrated, the white barbers didn't know how to cut black hair, so they had to bring in black barbers to show them. Someone from *Jet* magazine was there to take a picture." He pulled out a worn copy of *Jet*.

The way he engages with the space suggests a relaxed yet confident owner-ship. You can tell he belongs there because of the way he's touching the chair and the counter; he's in physical contact with his surroundings. This is one of the devices that makes the photograph believable—without knowing him, you believe Deas McNeil belongs to that barbershop. If you don't belong in a place, you don't touch anything because it's not yours. When you're making a portrait, let the subject touch something. Let them lean like they belong there. First I figured out where he should

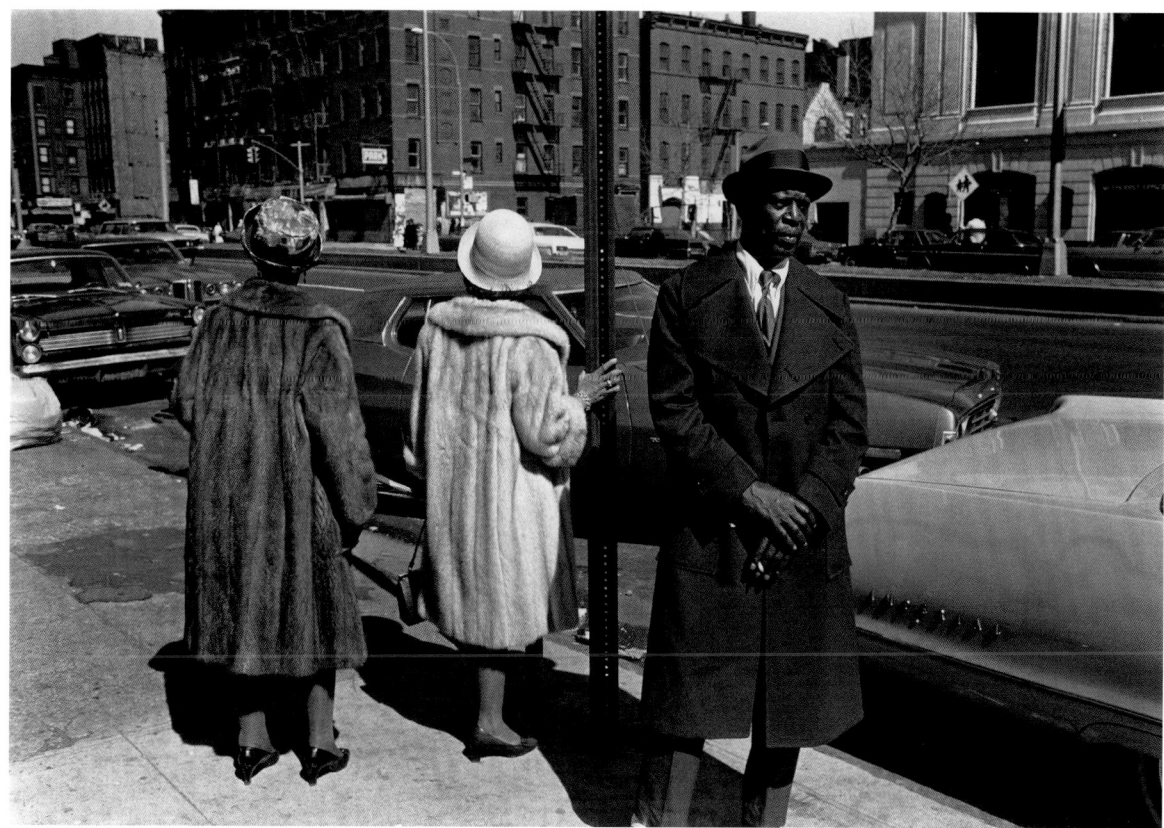

stand, using the mirror so the space wraps all the way around the picture, but that stance came from him. I can figure out the shape of the picture, but the subject's behavior is up to them.

Recently, I got a Facebook message from a woman asking if I was the same Dawoud Bey who had photographed her father in the 1970s. "I don't have any pictures of my father in his barbershop and when I saw your picture, I started crying." I sent her a print. That picture travels all the way from 1976 forward to now, forty-some years after it was made. It's one of the unintended ways that work continues to ripple in the world.

Above
Dawoud Bey
*A Man and Two Women After
a Church Service, Harlem*, 1976

Left
Dawoud Bey
*Deas McNeil, the Barber,
Harlem*, 1976

37

Once You Get There

I think all creative work is about the way in which your idea, the one that motivates you, brushes up against the actual situation.

When I began making those photographs on the streets of Harlem, my intentions were rather rhetorical. I wanted to create a positive view of the people of Harlem that would stand in opposition to the more pathological representations that had been constructed in the media. But once I began photographing, that preconceived notion had to give way to seeing what Harlem presented to me in reality, rather than validating something I thought I knew.

I've come to believe, from making photographs in Harlem all those years ago, that the best work tends to result not from the imposition of an idea on a situation, but from being responsive to what is going on once you get there. Otherwise, what results is merely the illustration of an idea. The idea is still meaningful, because it is the impetus that gets you out the door. But once you get there, the work has to be driven by the experiences you're actually having, the people you're actually meeting, and your best attempt of honestly and clearly describing these encounters. Hopefully, this process leads to something more than what you expected. That's what began to happen for me once I was in Harlem, not the hypothetical Harlem I had envisioned from Queens.

Right
Dawoud Bey
*A Woman and a Child in
the Doorway, Harlem,* 1975

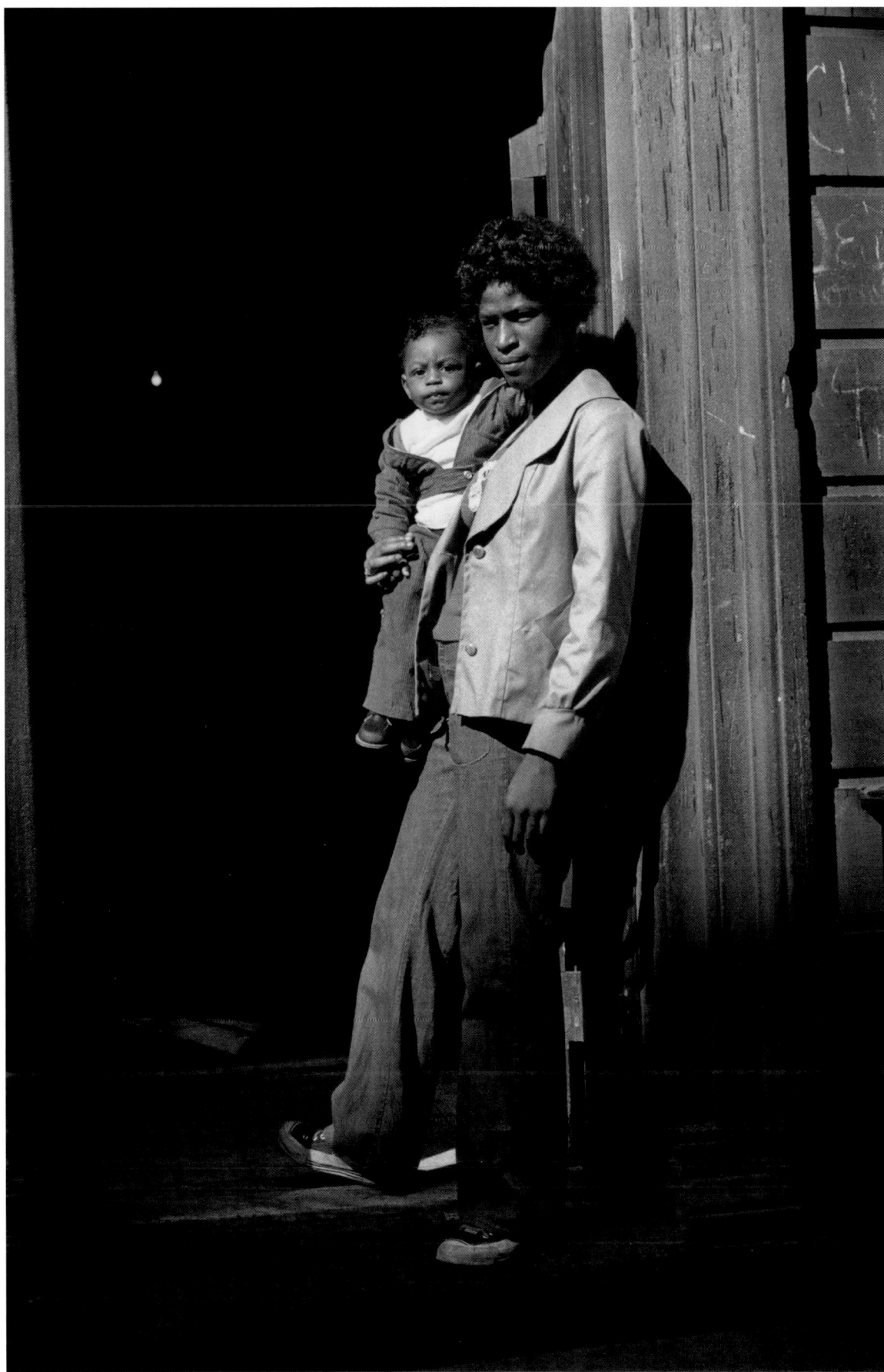

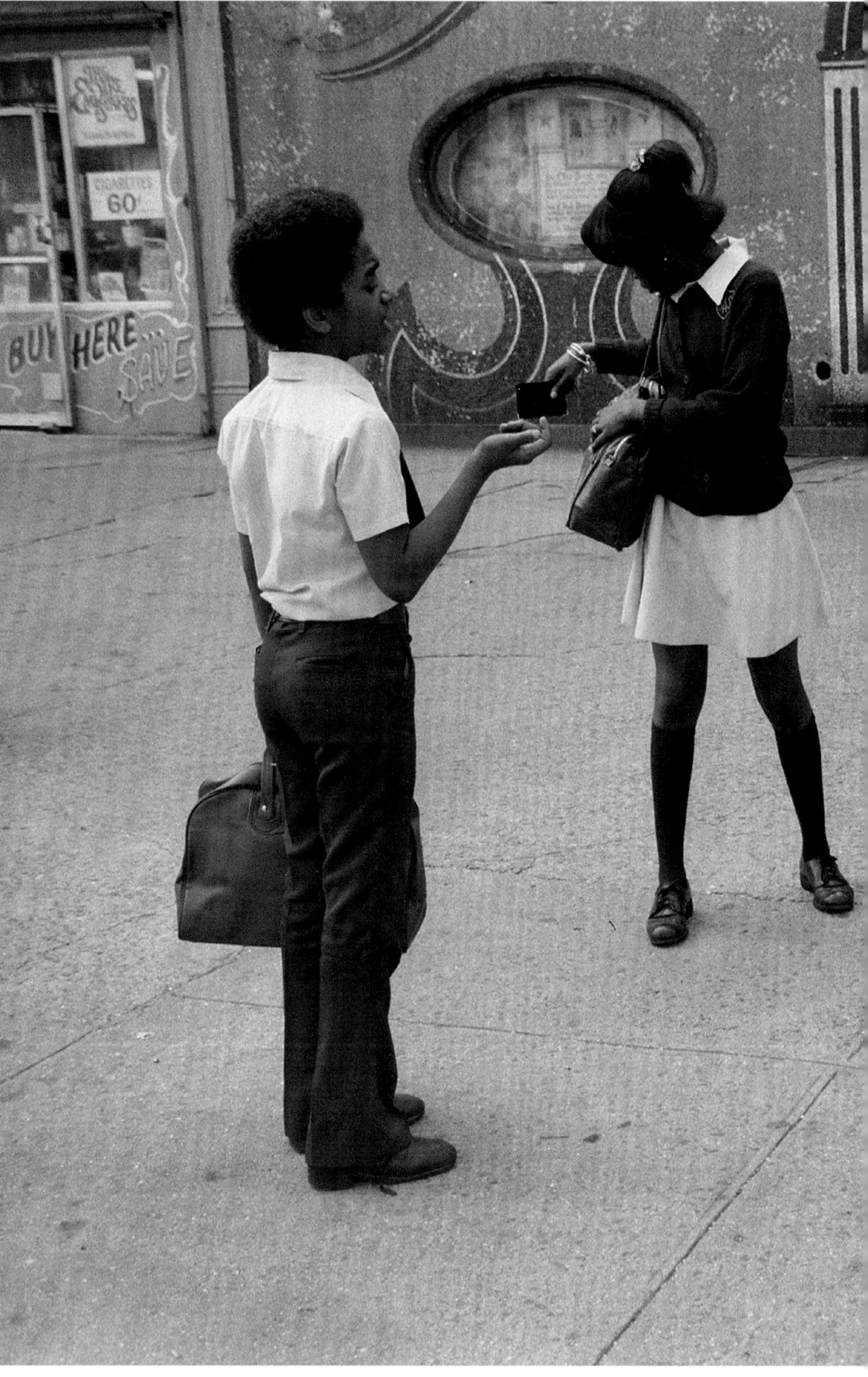

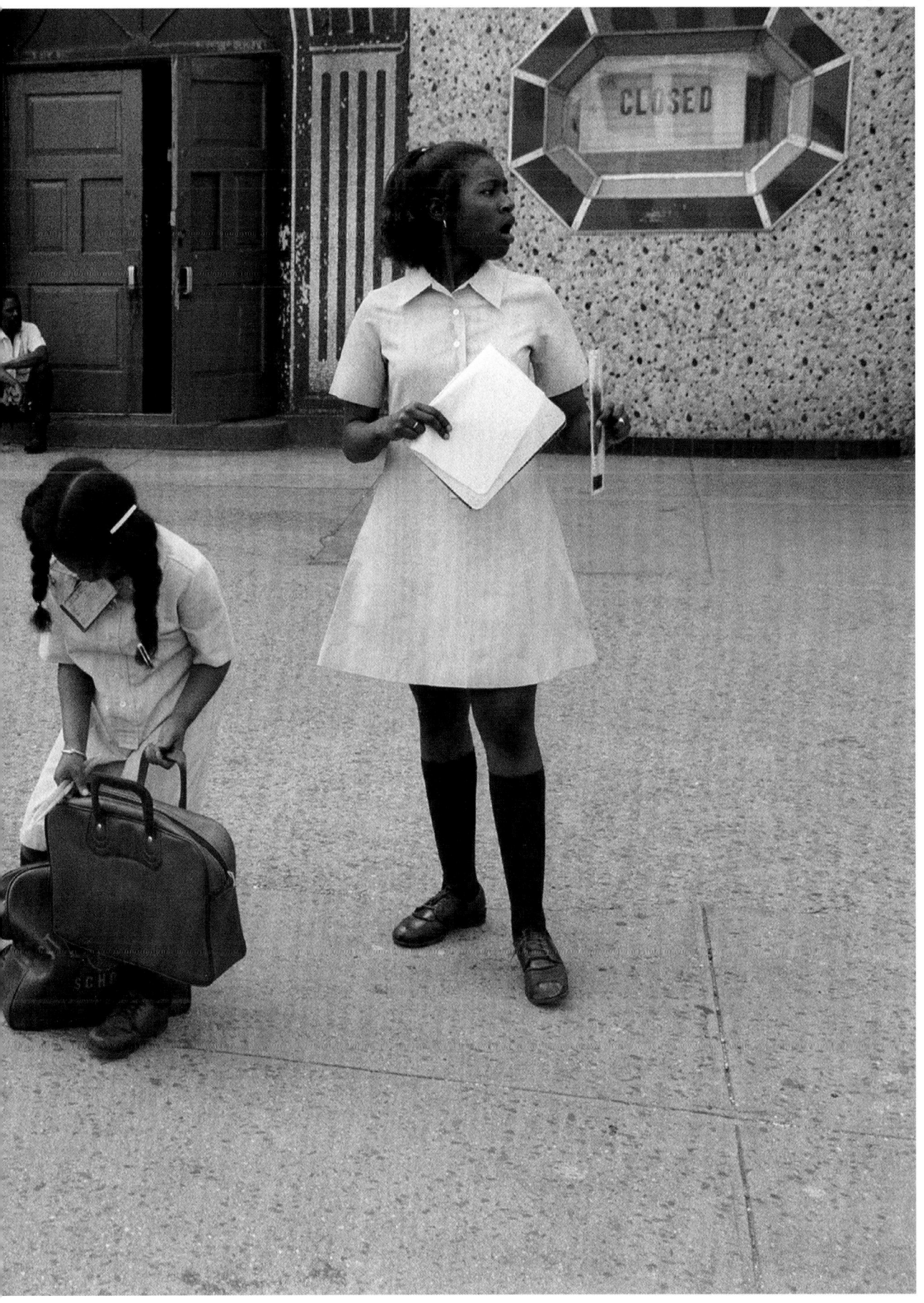

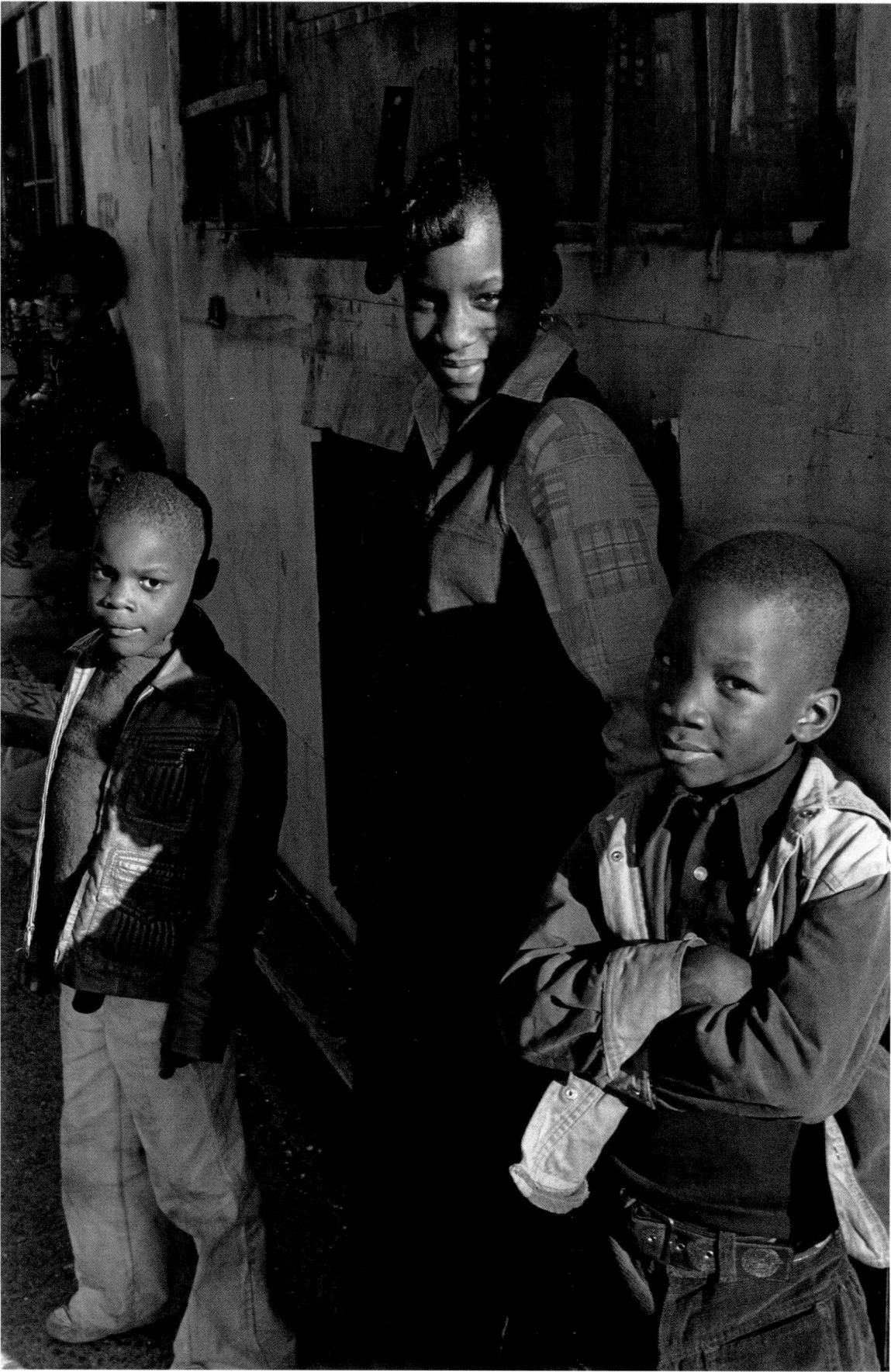

A photograph that migrates from a museum to a newspaper is still the same photograph, but the context changes both the audience and the nature of the conversation around the image.

Whether an image exists in an institutional space, or on a printed page, on social media, the context is an active and loaded site. Where the work is going to exist should always be part of the consideration in its making. What kind of conversation do you want the work to provoke?

Thinking back to my early experience of witnessing the protests surrounding *Harlem on My Mind* at the Met, I knew the institutional space of the museum was not benign. It could be a site of protest and also play an important role within the community where it sits. This shaped my thinking about where I wanted my work to end up. I knew I wanted my photographs on the walls of a museum; it was never my ambition for my work to be seen in magazines or newspapers.

I knew that I wanted to present my Harlem USA work in Harlem. I wanted to break the tradition of making the photographs in one place and showing them somewhere else, which can convey varying degrees of otherness in regards to the subject. I didn't want there to be a separation between subject and audience. I also didn't want to preclude the work going out into the world, but I thought it was important that it be shown in Harlem first. So I approached the Studio Museum in Harlem with the photographs I had made up to that point to see if they were interested in showing them. I had spent enough time at the museum and knew people there well enough to make an attempt. They were also the only museum in the Harlem community (this had everything to do with why they existed) so they were the most appropriate institution for my project. The exhibition opened in November of 1979.

Pages 40–41
Dawoud Bey
Four Children at Lenox Avenue, Harlem, 1977

Left
Dawoud Bey
Five Children, Harlem, ca. 1976

43

How does one get comfortable approaching a museum or an organization or a newspaper? It's the same as approaching a stranger to make a photograph: you just have to get used to it.

I recommend showing your work to as many people as possible, especially other photographers who have more experience than you do—establish an ongoing critical dialogue with them. Being part of a community of peers that are a half or full step ahead of you, who are doing the things that you want to do, can become a form of instruction. "Oh that's how you do that. You're showing them your portfolio? Who'd you talk to? Did they look at it? Really? Oh, Ok. Maybe I can show them mine." It is impossible to do good work and show it to a lot of people and not have something happen. You have to believe this.

If you are showing your work to informed viewers and no one is responding or talking up your work to other people, you need to take a long, hard look at your work. Don't be foolish enough to think you are right and everyone else is wrong. People I know who look at work—even with very different interests and tastes— tend to agree when something interesting comes along, and they tell others about it. I always talk to curators I know about new work I've seen, encouraging them to take a look at it. Usually, even if they are not able to do anything right away, they keep the work and the artist on their radar.

If you've been taking pictures for a while, you probably want to do some-thing with the work and you need to say what that is. Where do you hope to be in five years? Ten years? Dream out loud. If you find yourself being hesitant to say, it might be because you're afraid you won't be able to make it happen. But the fact of the matter is that it's impossible to get "there" without saying where it is you want to go. What you want will change over time, because you never really arrive, but there always has to be a *there*.

You also have to love the process of making the work, of getting *there*; it's the process that gets you to the achievement. Whatever success is going to happen will happen as a consequence of what you're making. You can't know what will come—the achievements don't exist before the work is made—so the process is all you have. There's never a point, as long as you're still breathing, when that's not how it is. You have to keep pushing, keep making your work.

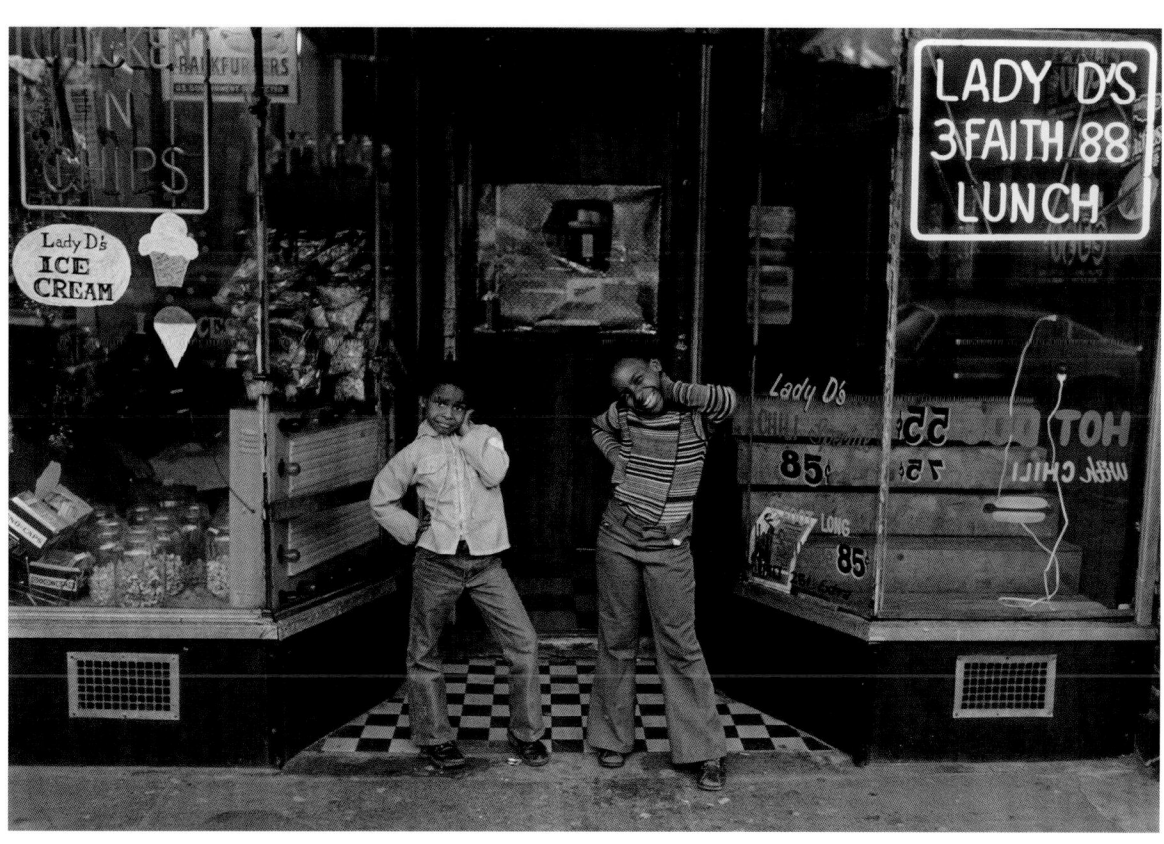

Dawoud Bey
Two Girls at Lady D's,
Harlem, 1976

A More Formal Portrait

Photography, perhaps more than any other medium, has always been tied to its technology—the object and the tools used to make that object are intimately related. Part of what I've done over the years is to find different ways to engage in the larger idea of visualizing the human subject in photographic form. The results and implications are dependent on the kind of tool, or camera, I use.

I made all of the Harlem work with a 35 mm camera. At that point, I didn't know that certain types of cameras are used to make certain types of pictures. I was working in a slow, deliberate way with a handheld camera that was better suited to photographing quickly and unobtrusively. There's a kind of stillness to the work, as if they were taken on a tripod, because those were the kinds of pictures I was looking at and wanted to emulate. It didn't occur to me that Avedon made his portraits with a view camera. I was actually using the 35 mm camera more like a large-format camera but was able to do so only up to a point. To make more formal portraits—ones that contained the kind of lush physical description I was looking for—I started to use a 4-by-5-inch camera.

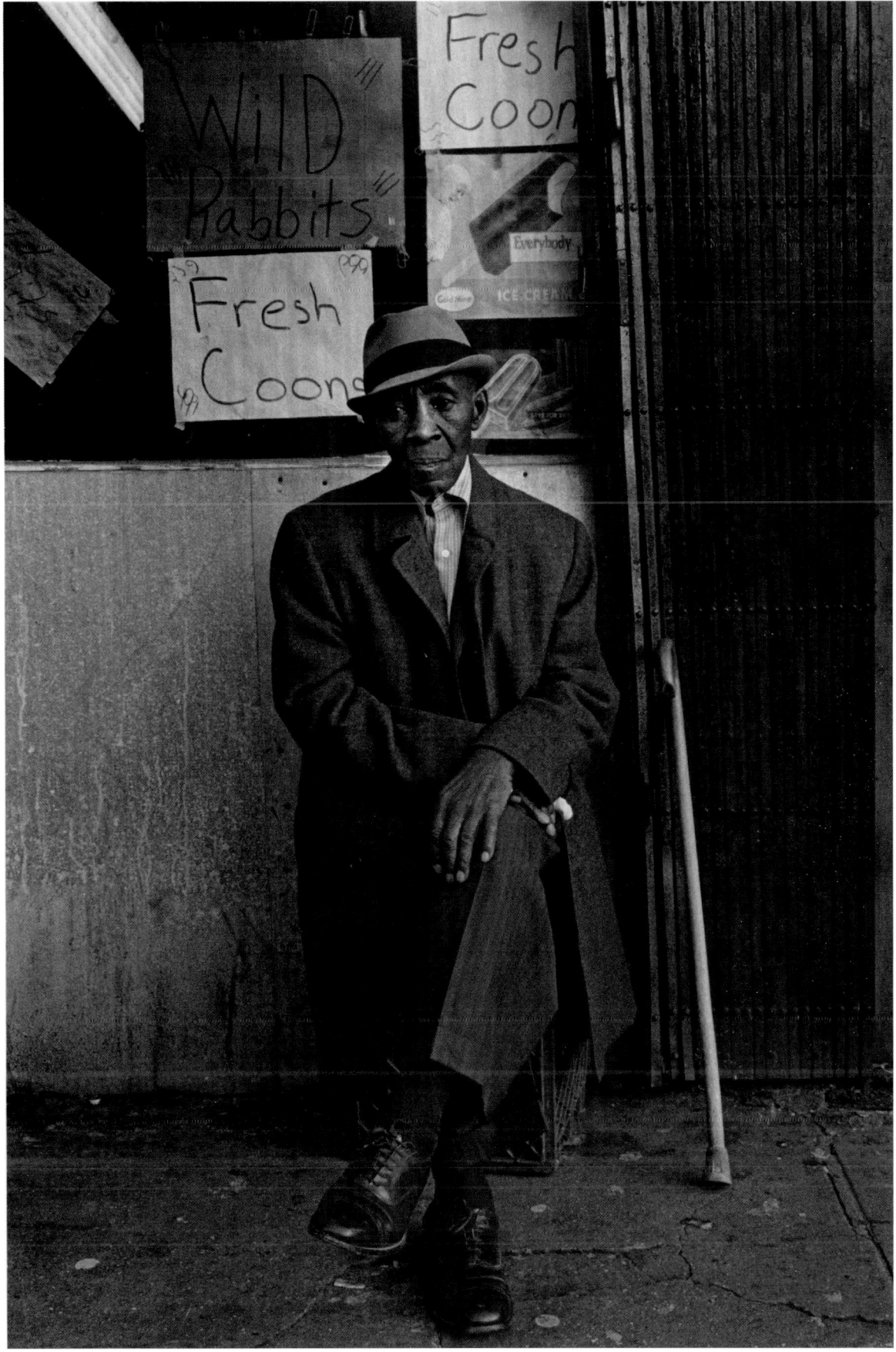

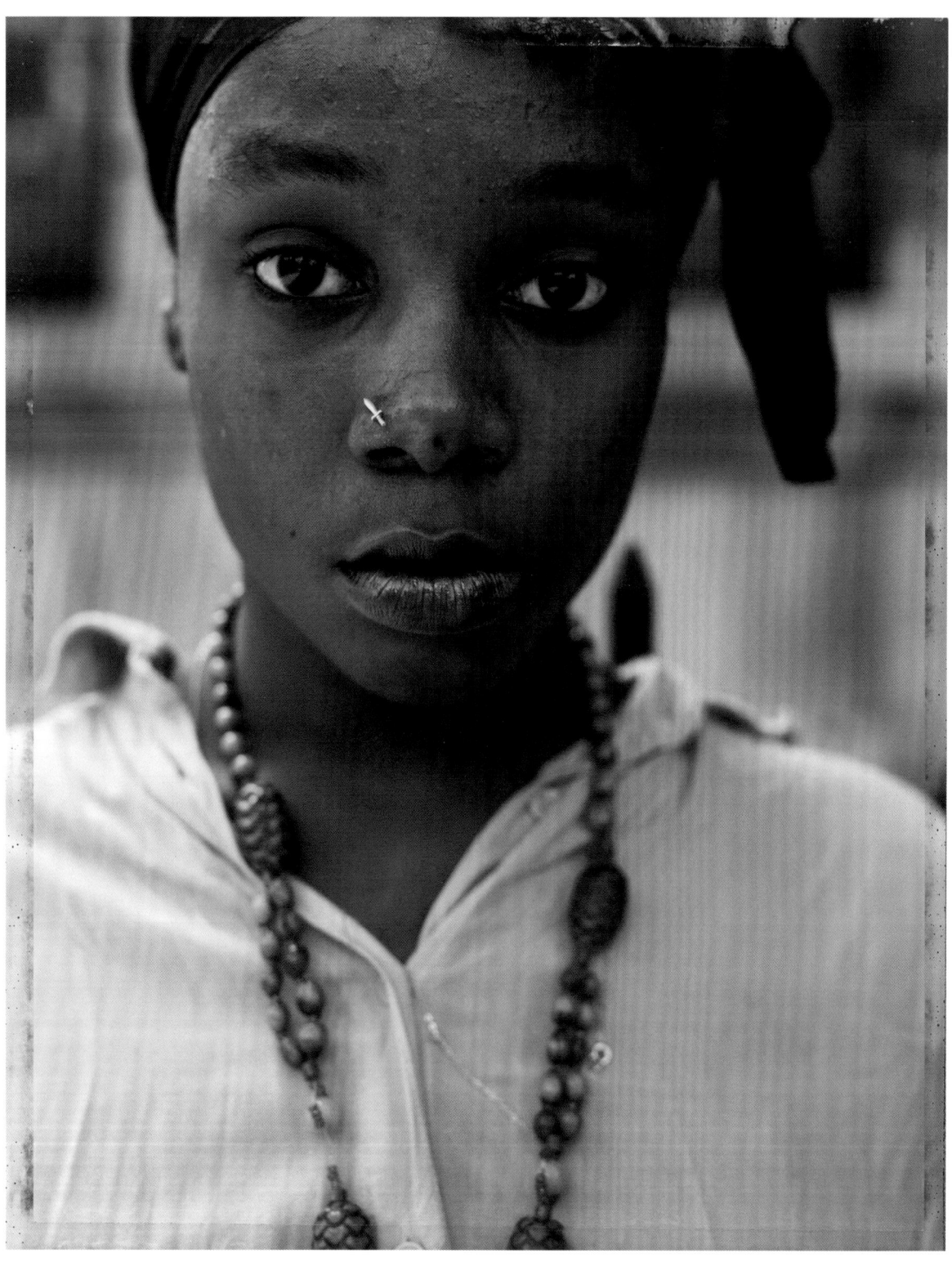

Dawoud Bey
A Girl with a Knife Nosepin,
Brooklyn, 1990

Photographer and Subject

Just as the quality of the picture changes with each camera, the relationship between you and the subjects changes as well. With a 4-by-5, I can control the photos in a much more intentional way: "You need to stand here because I'm going to set the tripod here." There's nothing spontaneous about it. Using a view camera on a tripod in the street lends an almost ceremonial atmosphere to the proceedings. It's very large and requires a different level of participation from both subject and photographer. I had to slow down the way I was making photographs.

Slowing down allowed for a much more collaborative process. Working in this way allowed me to confront the implicit hierarchy that I believe is established when you make photographs of people. That hierarchy privileges the photographer, who both makes and possesses the image. In a collaborative effort where subjects help shape how they are represented, they have more ownership of the space. I also started using Polaroid Type 55 film, which unfortunately no longer exists. That film created an instant print, which I gave to the subject, as well as a reusable negative, which I used to make the finished photographs. Part of shifting from the 35 mm camera to the 4-by-5 was to deepen and extend my engagement with the person I was photographing. I wanted to see if I could chart a path that made use of photography's documentary tradition and also addressed the tensions between photographer and subject.

Walking around with the 4-by-5 camera and a tripod, I began photographing in the neighborhood I was living in at that time, Brooklyn, and later in Washington, DC, and Rochester, New York. I continued to photograph African American subjects; it was part of my agenda to make the black subject a visible presence in my photographs, and in doing so, give them a presence in the tradition I was working within and ultimately a place on the walls of galleries and museums when the work would be exhibited.

There's an amplification in this photograph that's both material, from the larger negative, and optical, from the lens of the camera. The larger negative is more descriptive: You can see everything—the tie, the clasp, the skin. The optical quality of the 4-by-5 camera allowed me to use a shallow depth of field to push the subject more into the space of the viewer while still relying on that heightened quality of description. The backgrounds are hardly ever sharp in these photographs. There's just enough focus for you to see it, but the main focus is on the subject.

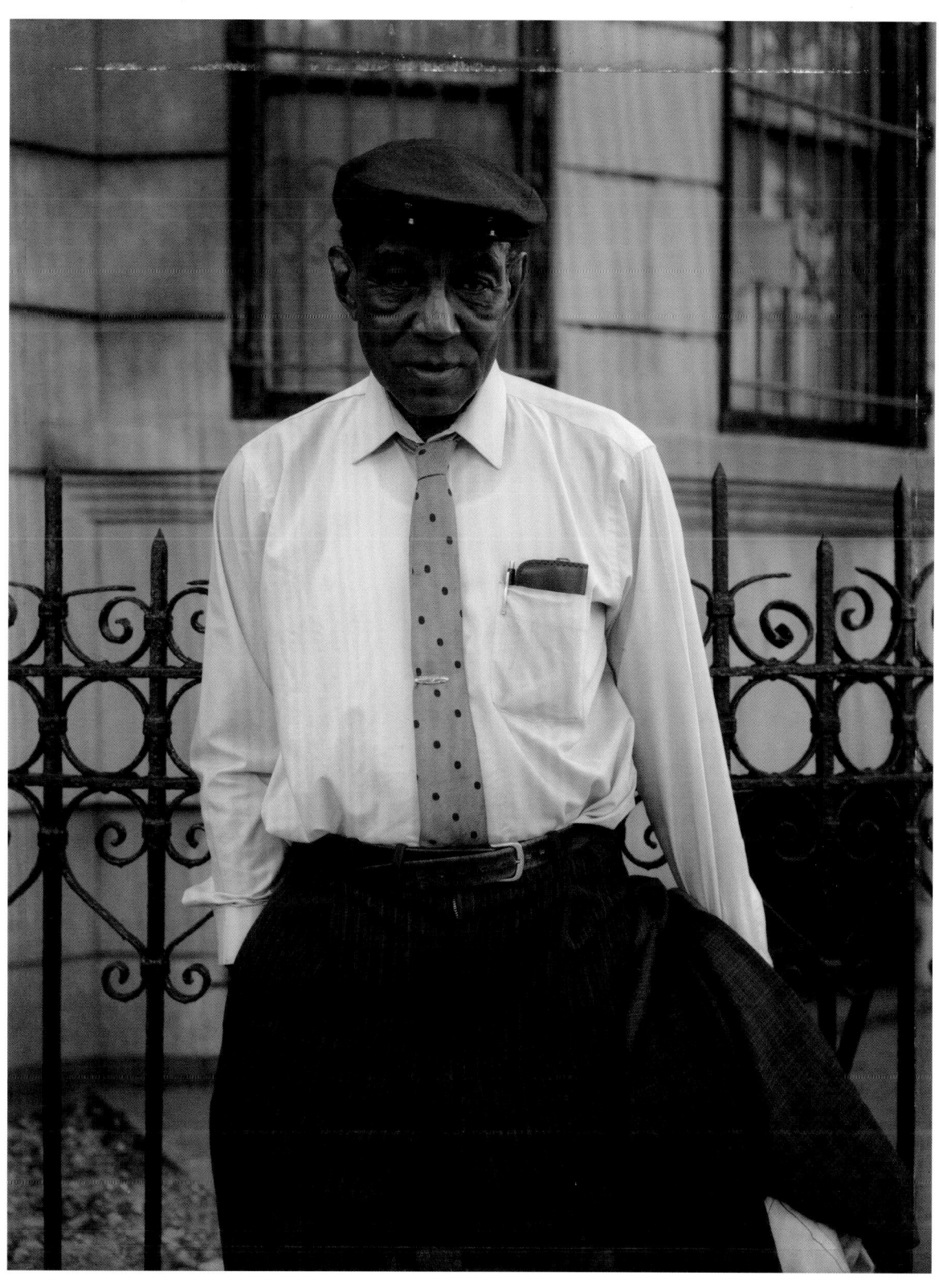

Dawoud Bey
A Man on the Way to the Cleaners,
Brooklyn, 1990

Space to Be Themselves

I saw this couple walking toward me in the park. I was already set up and waiting for someone to come by. If you take them out and look at the shape of the picture—the slanted tree, the hanging leaves, and the lines framing the open space—I just needed people to put there. So I asked the couple, "Do you mind if I make a picture of you? I'll give you one." They said yes, and then we began to put their pose and picture together. When I ask people to pose for me, I always allow them to make the first gesture. I just say, "Make yourself comfortable," and then whatever they do, that's the beginning of working their gestures into something that I think invokes a compelling sense of presence.

They stood there together, and I said something like, "Well, you can act like you know each other!" I didn't know what they were going to do after that, but I knew they were going to do *something*. I worked from there. I might have said, "Pull a little closer" or, "Turn this way." Again, I didn't know how they were going to do this, but I gave them the space, hoping it would work out.

You have to give people the space to perform their own behavior because as one of my favorite teachers in grad school, Richard Benson, used to say, "The things that are going on in the world are so much more interesting than anything you can make up." It's true.

If the pose comes from the subject, it will ring truer than anything I could direct. I can't anticipate subtleties like the drape of her hand or the placement of his hand—the little poetic gestures or grace notes. I have to let them evolve and then recognize them when I see them, like the slight raising of her head: "That's great. Just hold that and look at the camera." This takes time, so they get comfortable, and their gestures become more relaxed as they become more sustained. I look for *how* they are through their own gestures and dispositions, which help me make the photograph I can only imagine.

I'm also figuring out exactly where the picture begins and ends. Here, I decided that it should begin at the bottom of the dress, so I probably backed up a little bit to make sure I didn't cut it off. And the picture needs to end at the top of his cap. While they were posing I realized that there was a little too much empty space. The picture needed something else. I noticed people riding their bikes to the right and thought they would fill in the space nicely. I'm looking at the couple, but I'm also waiting for the bicycles to come into the frame. It's funny because I can't tell them, "Hey, just hold it because I'm waiting for something to fill in that space." I'm just hoping the bikes go by soon. It's all about being responsive to the shape of the things in front of you. You don't want to disrupt the form of the content. You have to be able to see deeply.

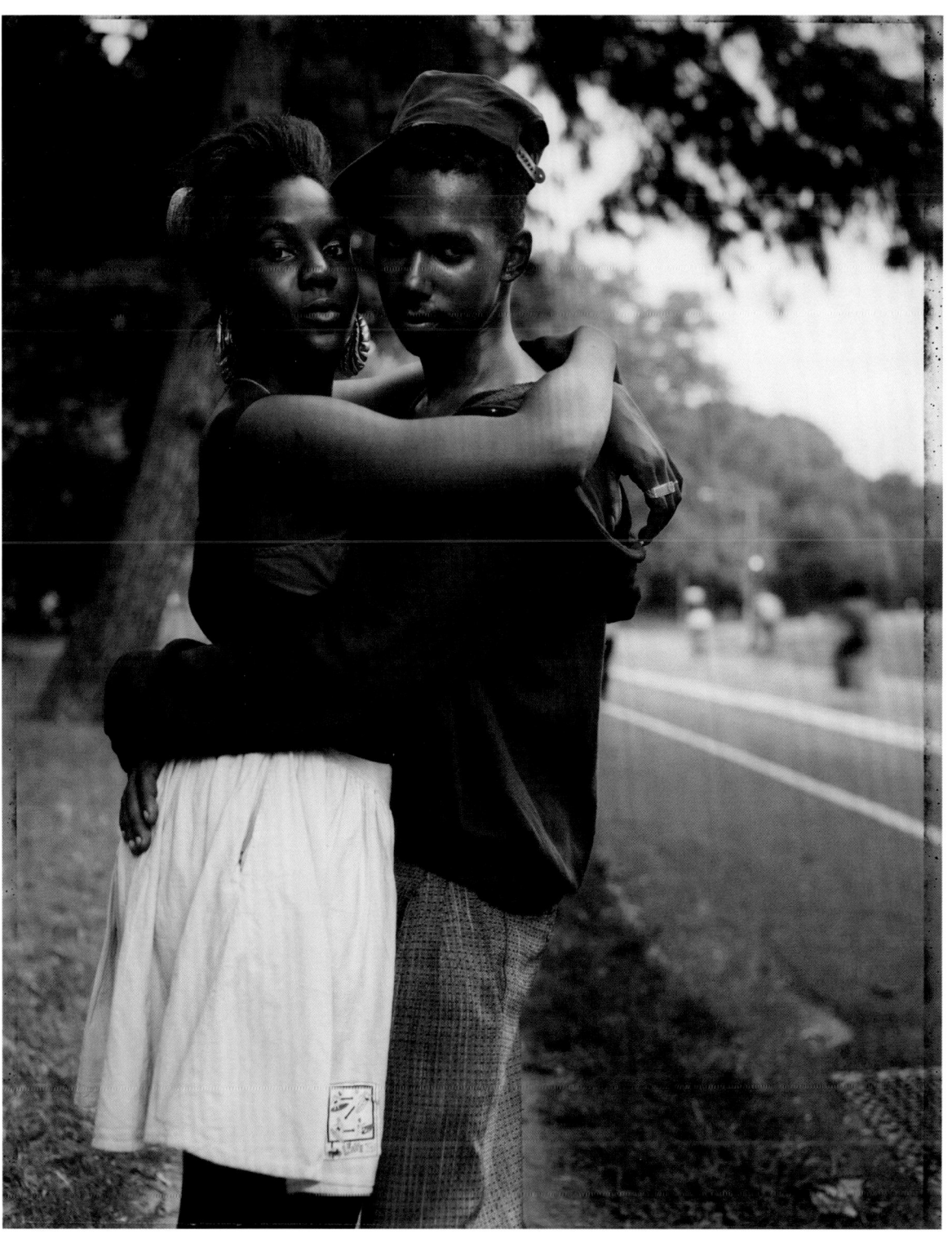

Dawoud Bey
A Couple in Prospect Park,
Brooklyn, 1990

53

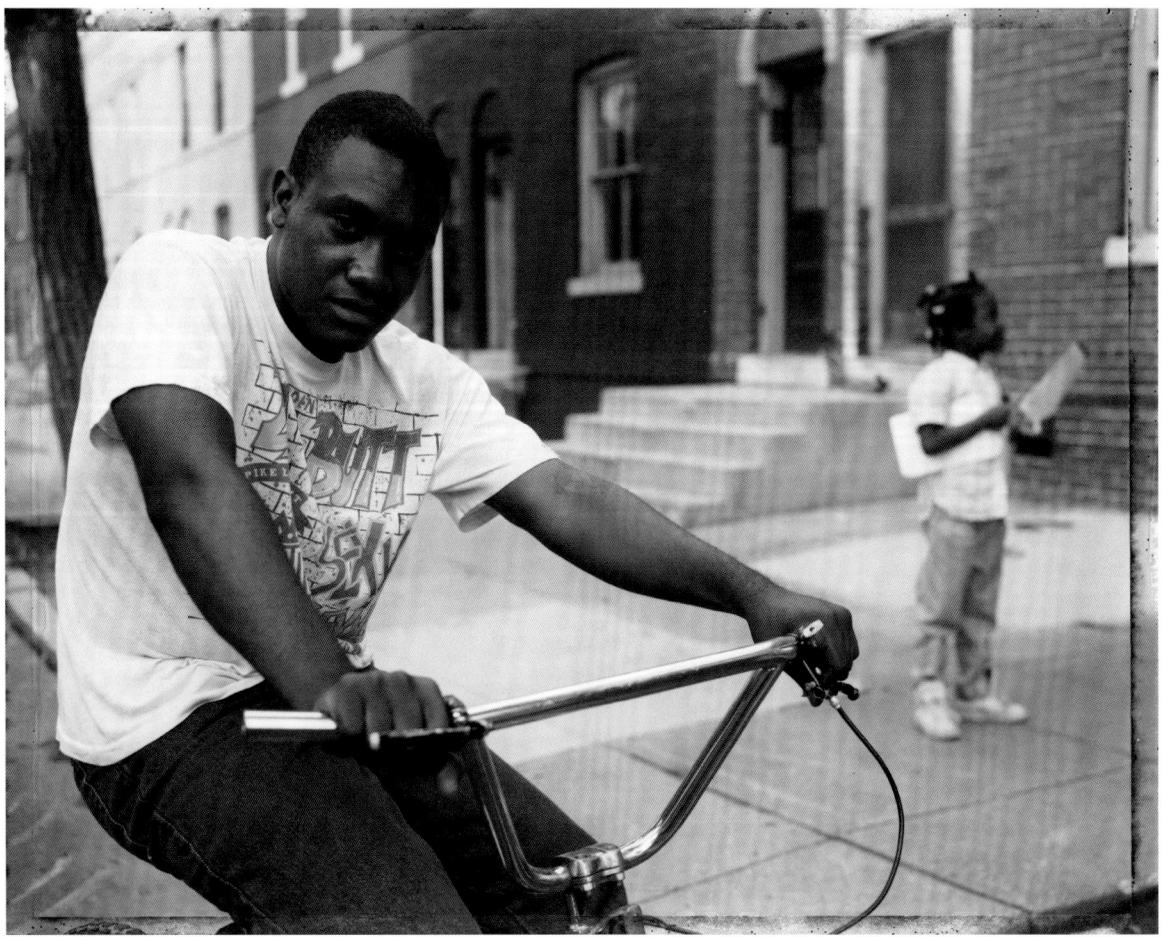

When I stopped this boy on the bike for a portrait, he was very skeptical, but I told him I was going to give him the picture. While I was talking to him, I saw this little girl talking to her mother off camera, so I asked the boy to roll the bike toward me. I'm trying to get the two of them in the same space. I'm thinking about her, but I'm really working with him. Once, he's in place, I have to work quickly because I don't know if she'll move or he'll get restless.

While these pictures are staged, I want the viewer to believe this is a casual encounter or everyday experience. The portraits have this informal quality because they're made on the street, but there's nothing casual about them. I direct people toward this appearance of informality so that you can believe what you see in the photograph is something true about them.

I say the "appearance" of informality, of the subject being at ease, because I don't know what's going on internally for them. I never ask, "What are you thinking about as you're gazing into the lens?" because I'm more interested in what they look like as they're doing it. They may be thinking any number of things and sometimes even a little uneasiness can translate well psychologically in front of the camera.

Dawoud Bey
A Young Man on a Bike,
Washington, DC, 1989

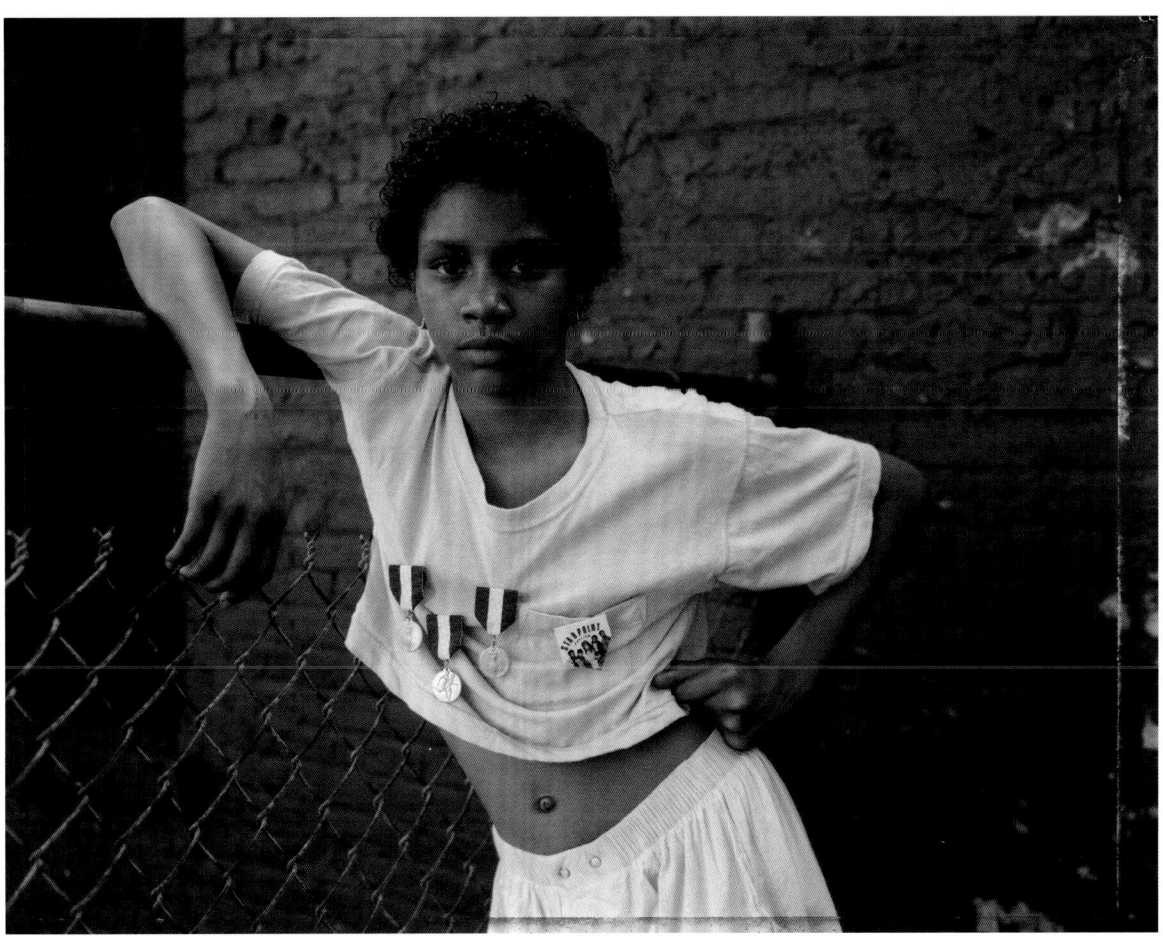

You can sense that the guy on the bike is skeptical from his expression. He looks like he might ride off at any minute. He went along with it, but we weren't going to be fist bumping at the end. And that's fine. All I needed him to do was be present. The girl above, on the other hand, was walking around with her school medals on. She obviously wanted everyone to see her accomplishments, and I gave her an opportunity to really be seen. She was proud, and you can see that in the picture.

The portrait is something of a performance, and what I'm trying to do, with a very subtle hand, is direct them to a heightened performance of themselves. I know that her gaze toward the camera ultimately translates to the gaze toward the viewer. I want her to appear as if she is being herself so that when viewers look at the picture they will feel like they know something about her, even though that's impossible. You can't truly know something about a person from a flat, still representation, but if a picture successfully conveys the powerful psychology of body language and expression, it has the capacity to allow us to momentarily enter the life of a stranger.

Dawoud Bey
*A Girl with School Medals,
Brooklyn,* 1988

55

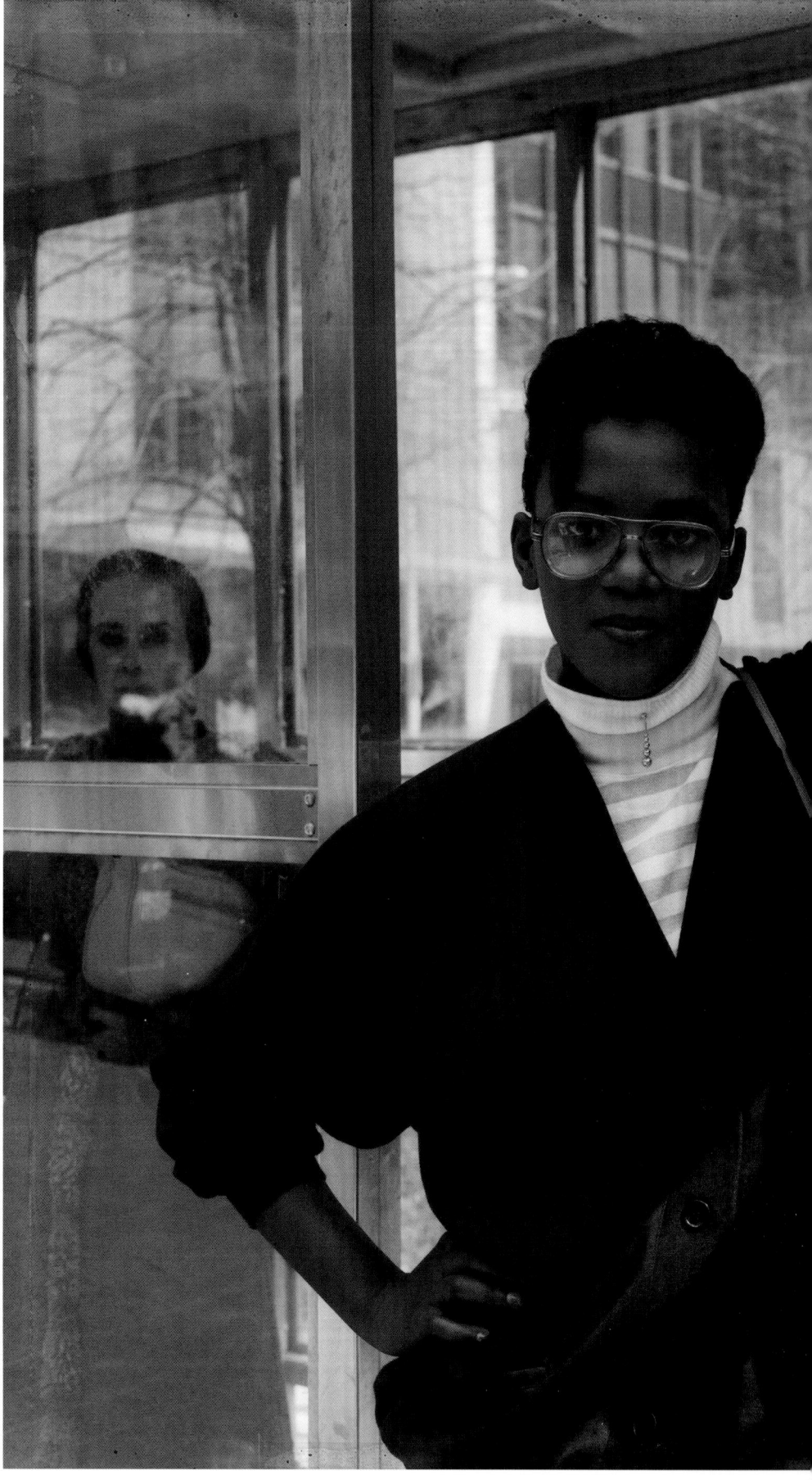

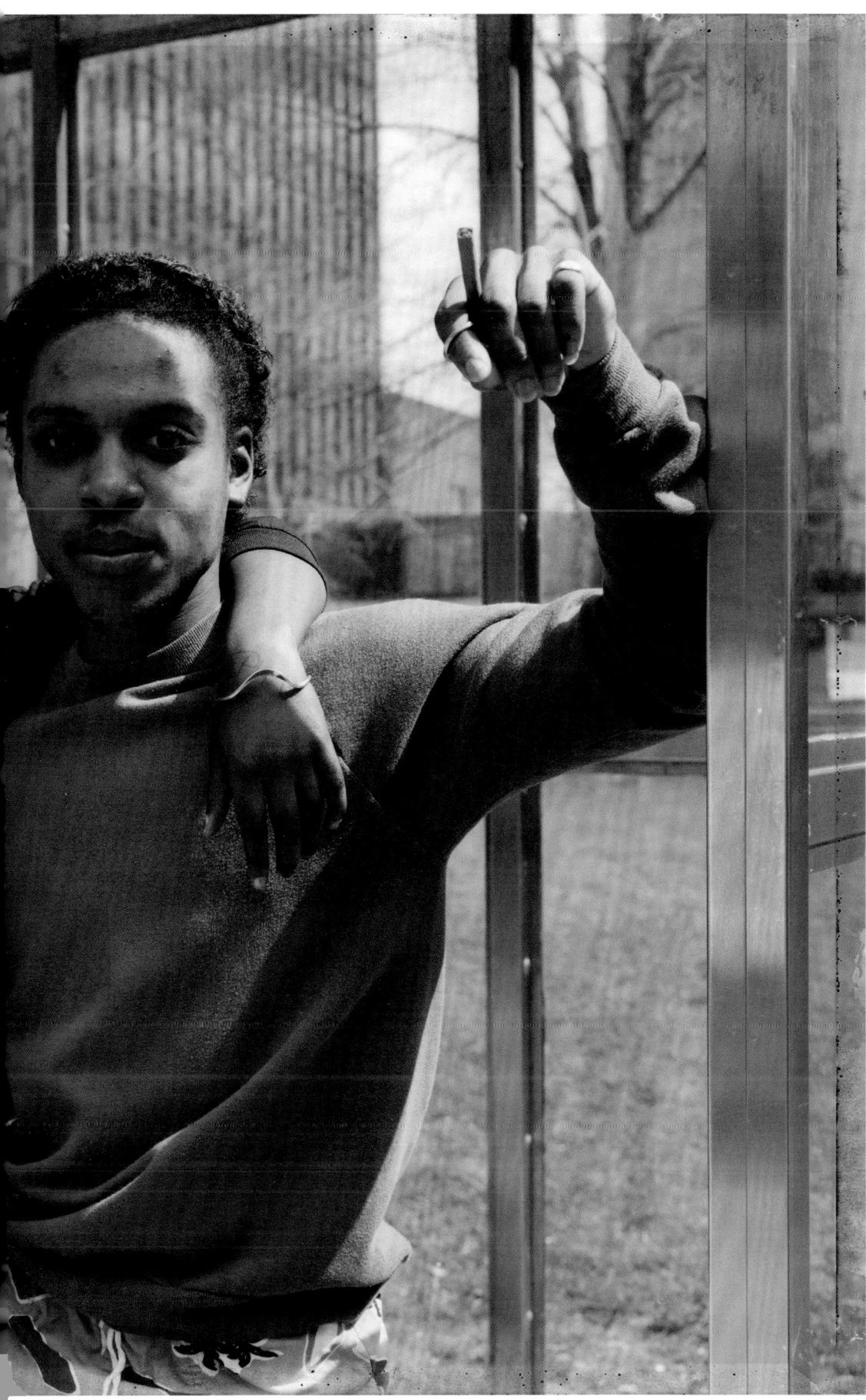

A More Extended Statement

Pictures have to hold their own as pictures, but they also have a relationship to other images as a project or series deepens. Each picture builds on an idea to form the larger project. Together, the individual photographs add up to a more extended statement about the community.

I'm conscious from the outset that I'm making a body of work, a group of photographs meant to be seen together, so there has to be both range and coherence. Even as you're working with the same ideas, the same subjects, the same community, how do you avoid making the same photograph over and over? How do you keep revisiting an idea, but shape it at the same time? Being mindful of repetition is a start. Keep expanding your possible ways to realize the work, thinking, "How else can I approach this?"

I remember when I was starting this body of work, I showed it to a curator. At the end of the portfolio, he said, "This is really powerful work, just watch out for the hands on the hips." It's true that most people, left to their own devices, are going to put their hands on their hips or their hands in their pockets. It took him calling this to my attention to realize that I probably had enough of these pictures, that I had to be more inventive. You have to change up the way you make pictures so they result in something more varied, so that they're not all made from the same vantage point or subject-to-camera distance. When making photographs of people, you have from close up to full body to everything in between; use it.

Pages 56–57
Dawoud Bey
A Couple at a Main Street Bus Stop,
Rochester, New York, 1989

Right
Dawoud Bey
A Young Woman Between Carrolburg Place
and Half Street, Washington, DC, 1989

58

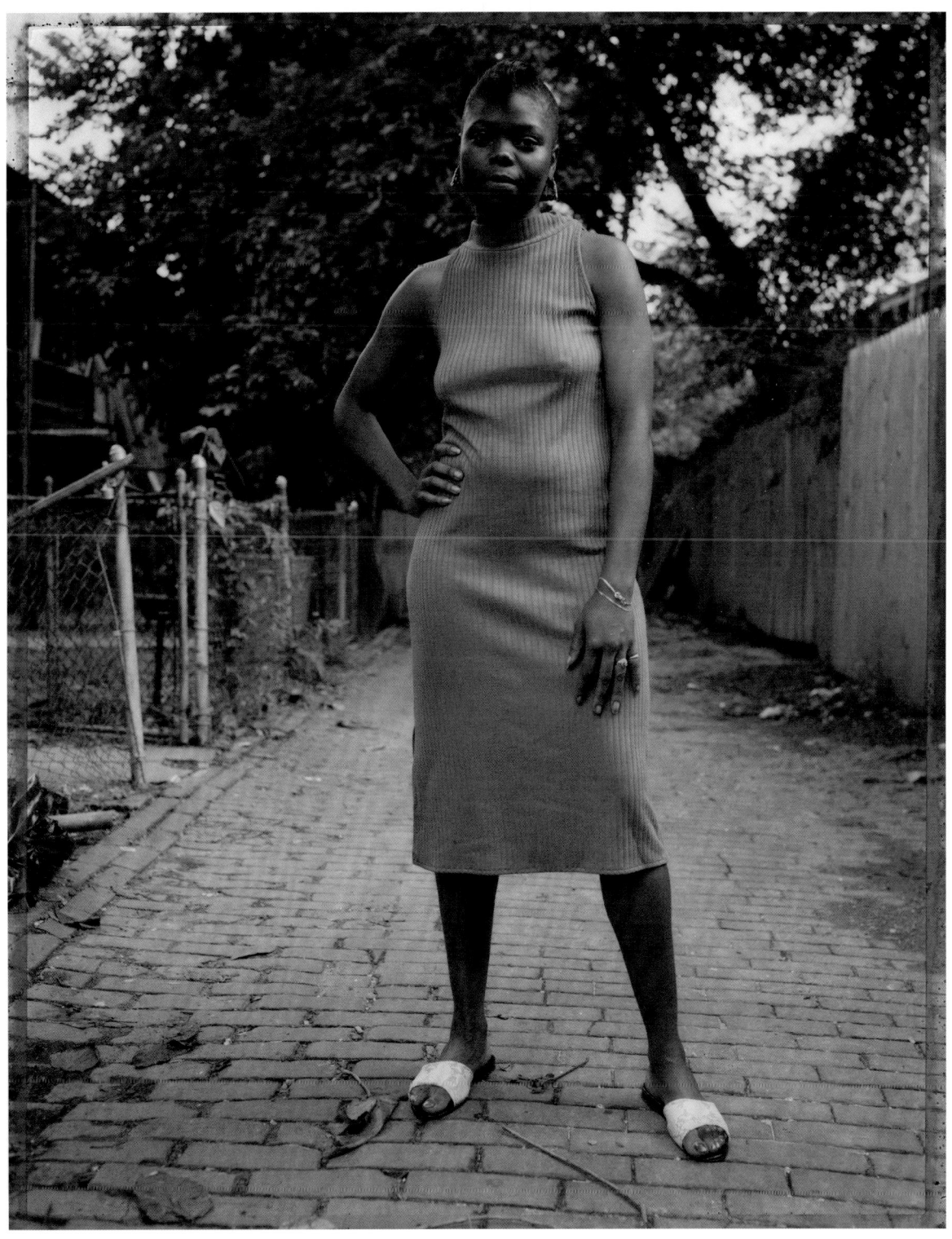

I have a fundamental curiosity about the human subject, especially about people who have been marginalized. I believe that through making pictures there's a chance viewers will become invested in these subjects too.

Because I've chosen the camera as my means to do this, I'm compelled to make sure my photographs are their most resonant. Otherwise, why the camera? I could write, which I also do. But if you're going to use the camera, it requires that you be equally invested in the means of production as you are in the subject.

The Harlem pictures were small photographs, printed at 6 by 9 inches. I wanted the experience of looking at them to be intimate. When images are printed small, it's clear they're photographic objects. It's not the thing itself, but a picture of it, as opposed to larger photographs, which become more of an experience than an object. Of course, it is still an object, a large photographic object, but under the right circumstances, the shift in scale allows the viewer to feel like they're in the photograph. With a smaller-scale print, you really have to press your nose to it to enter into the picture. You're always conscious of the object—the pictureness— as opposed to almost involuntarily entering into what's being described.

Initially, I printed these at 20 by 24 inches, which was a huge leap in scale. I went from very small objects to nearly life-size ones. Now I'm printing these portraits at 32 by 40 inches, and I feel they're being fully realized for the first time; they finally have the kind of presence I always wanted them to have. These formal but casual street portraits become a space for black subjects to assert themselves in the world, with their gaze meeting the viewer's on an equal footing. It is important to me that the photograph projects itself into the viewer's space.

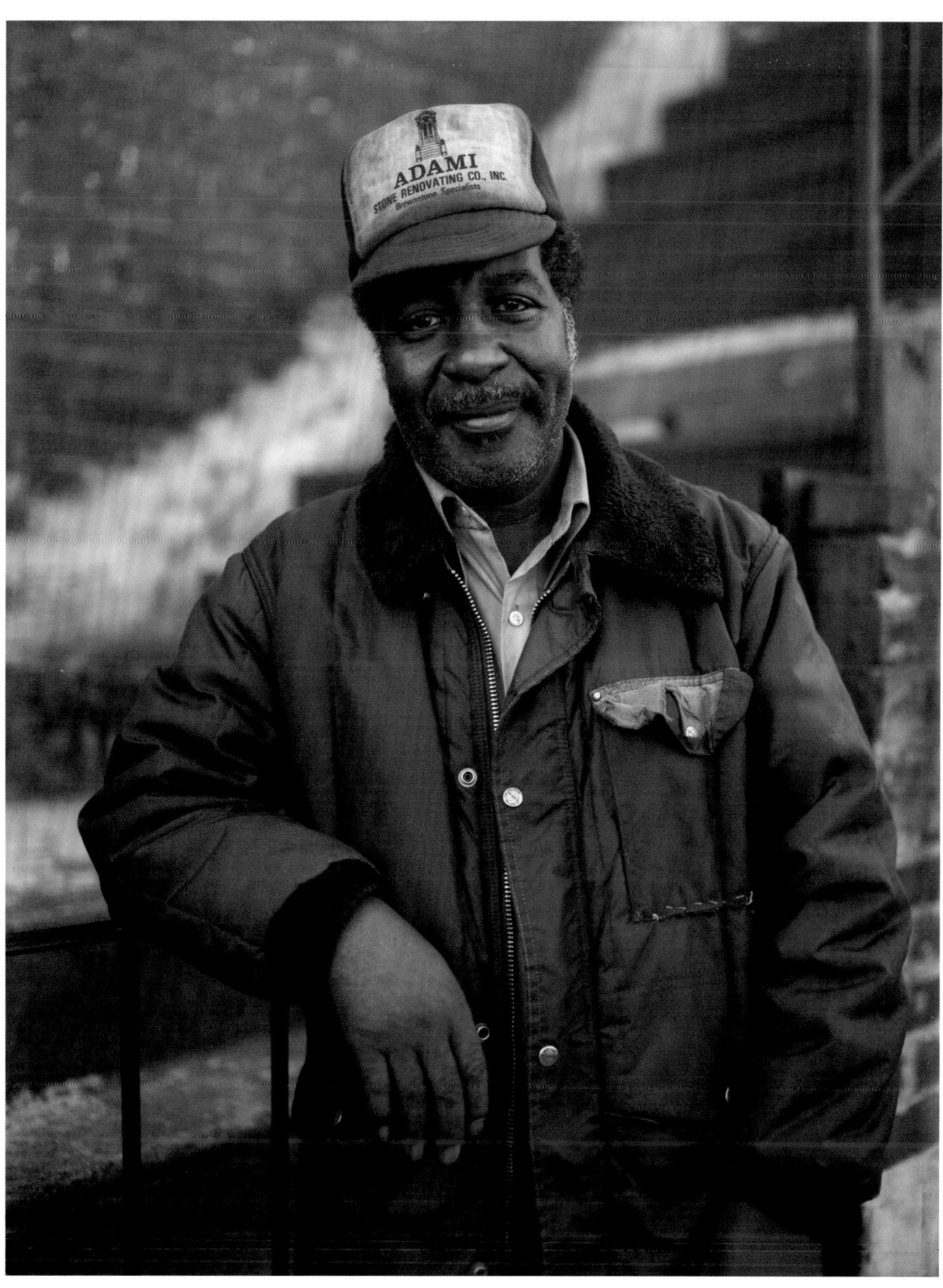

Dawoud Bey
A Man Wearing an Adami Cap,
Brooklyn, 1988

Unmooring the Subject

I had been making formal portraits in the environment of the street since I started, but I wanted to see what happened if I removed subjects from their environment. I wanted to make work that was less socially determined, to unmoor subjects from the social space of the background and situate them in the neutral space of the studio, where the narrative of the picture rested solely on their appearance.

I had been using Polaroid's Type 55 film as part of their then-existent Polaroid Artists Support Program, in which they sent me film in exchange for images for their collection. Polaroid also operated a 20-by-24-inch camera, and I applied for time to work with it in their studio. They gave you a day in the studio in return for two photographs from that day's work. So in 1991, I began working in the Polaroid studio in New York, initially making photographs of artist friends of mine who I asked to sit for formal portraits. I spent the next ten years making pictures with the 20-by-24 Polaroid view camera exclusively.

That's often how opportunities come about; you try to form relationships with institutions and the people there based on your own practice and then build upon those relationships organically. You're part of each other's community. It's important to keep in touch with people, even when it doesn't look like they can do anything for you. Form a community, rather than a "network." I have had numerous exhibitions and other opportunities result from keeping in touch with people, sometimes for up to ten years. People can often be interested in your work, but it takes time for the right situation to develop where they can do something with it. They may not be ready to commit right away because they need to see what you're going to do next. That's part of what they're investing in—they want to know that you are in it for the long haul. The last thing they want to do is make an early commitment to someone who decides to give it up.

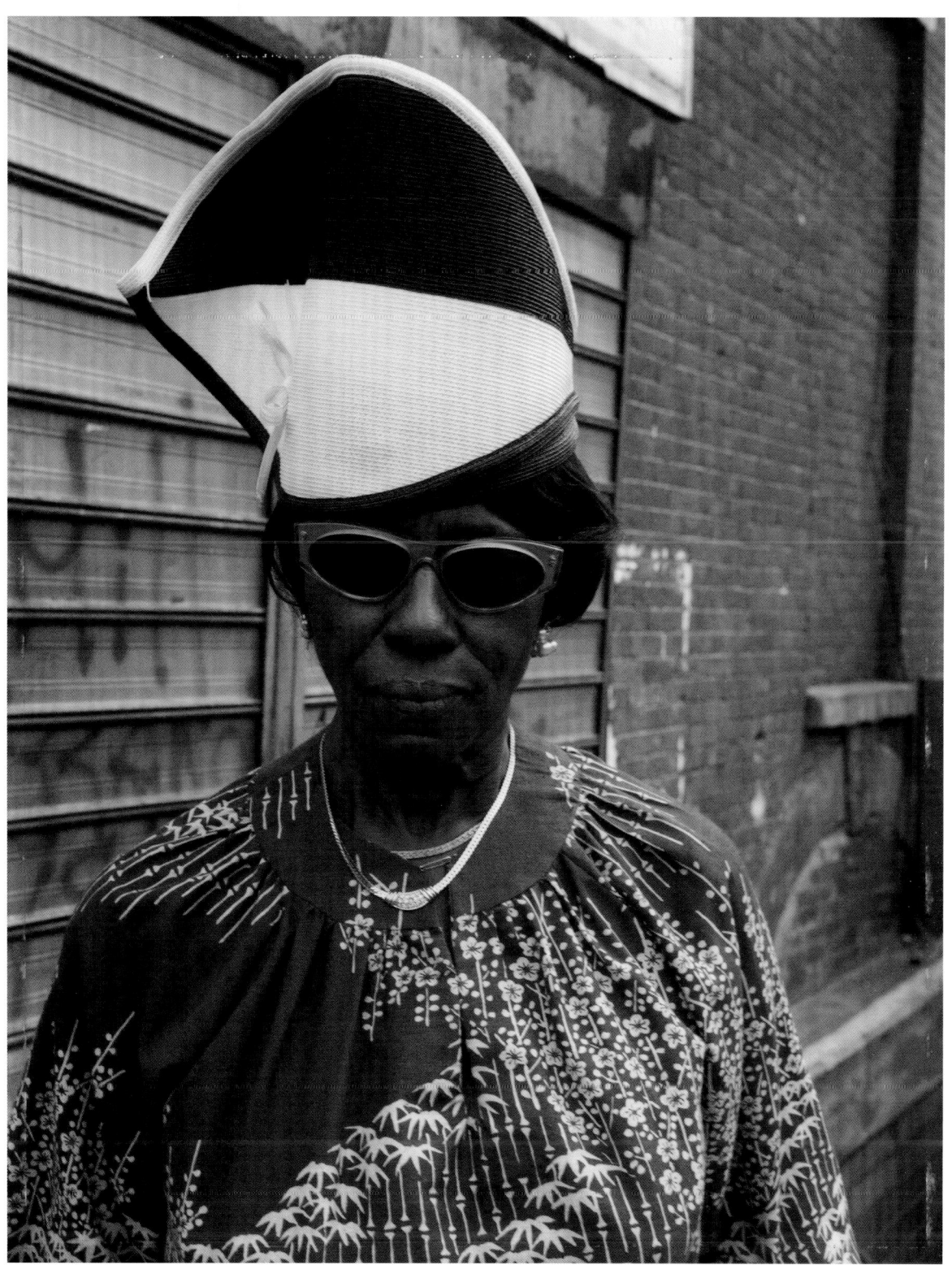

Dawoud Bey
*A Woman at Fulton Street
and Washington Avenue,
Brooklyn*, 1988

When I was asked to write a report on Rembrandt in the sixth grade, I fell in love with his paintings. All the years I was working in black and white on the street, I wasn't able to make direct use of that influence, but when I started photographing in the 20-by-24 studio, I decided to work in color.

Part of that decision was a desire to move away from a documentary tradition of making pictures—long implied by working in black and white. Color adds a degree of material specificity to the description of a subject that makes the experience of the person more palpable and immediate. Because of the view camera's sheer size, it reveals more detail than we can see with the naked eye and produces pictures that are hyperreal. This gives the subject a monumental presence in the space.

When I started making photographs in the Polaroid studio, Rembrandt was my point of reference—his heightened sense of the physical and psychological, the warm background, the monumental subject, and dramatic lighting. I wanted to bring those classic devices to contemporary subjects, my subjects.

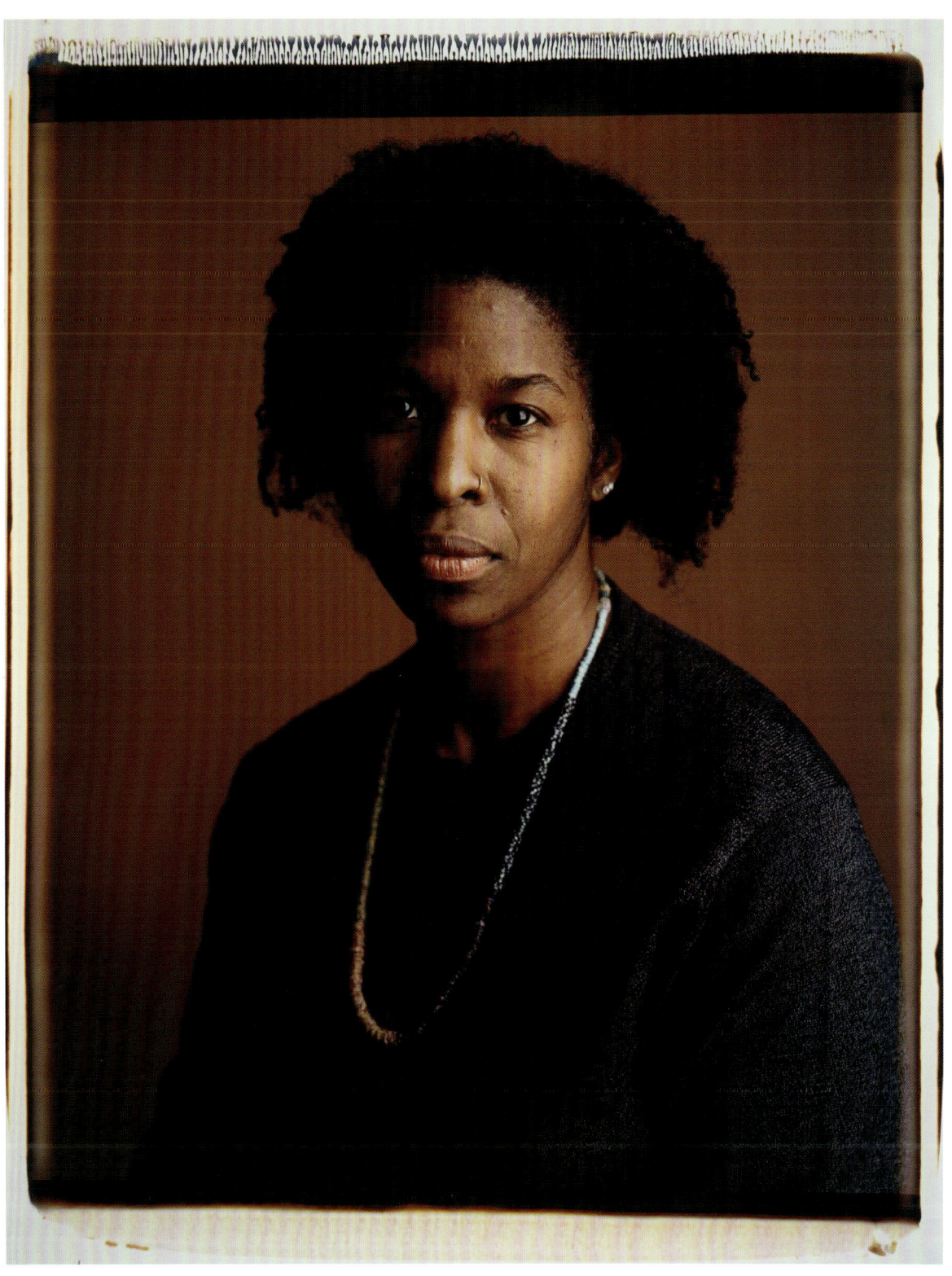

Dawoud Bey
Cheryl, New York, 1991

A Simple Setup

As I walked into the Polaroid studio on that first day, I wondered what I had gotten myself into, photographing with a 265-pound camera on wheels. I was immediately hit with a barrage of questions: What color backdrop did I want to use? What kind of lighting setup? The list of possibilities was extensive: lights in soft boxes suspended from the ceiling, light stands, umbrellas, snoots, barn doors, flags, and a seemingly endless assortment of seamless color paper.

I wanted to keep it simple and had Rembrandt in mind, so I chose a setup with one main light diffused through a soft box and another light on the backdrop, for which I chose a shade of brown, figuring it would work well with the range of people I was planning to photograph that first day. I didn't want the lighting to over-power the person and become too theatrical, or the background to be too distract-ing. I wanted to create a warm quiet space. I still use this basic setup for nearly all of my portrait work, inside or outside the studio: a single strobe, an umbrella or a soft box, and a view camera. I add a backdrop and an additional light in a studio setting.

It helped to have a starting point before I got to the studio so I wasn't comple-tely adrift in the space. The only way to get through that technical frustration and learning curve is to know what it is you want to do with the equipment. Then it all starts to make sense: "How do I get the camera and the lights to do *this*?" If there's no "this," how do you even begin?

When it comes to lighting, forget about the rules and what you're supposed to do, just look at the subject and move the light; when you see the effect you're looking for, that's where the light goes. If it's too harsh, you need to diffuse it, either bouncing it off an umbrella or through an umbrella. Try them both and see what it looks like. Then make that your lighting. It's hard to make these decisions if you don't have an idea going in. Otherwise, you could be experimenting for the next six months to learn what the gear does, when quite frankly, you really only need to know how it all works in relation to a very specific need. It's about making the pictures, not using the gear. You can learn more about technical options when you want to make something different. Once I made the first exposure with the soft box and saw what it looked like, I was like, "Oh, that's perfect. That's it." It looked exactly as I wanted it to look.

Once you figure out what lighting works, what backdrop works, those de-cisions are made; just start making the work. Take all that other stuff, pack it up, and put it away. They're just distractions. You need to stay focused on what matters: the person in front of the camera.

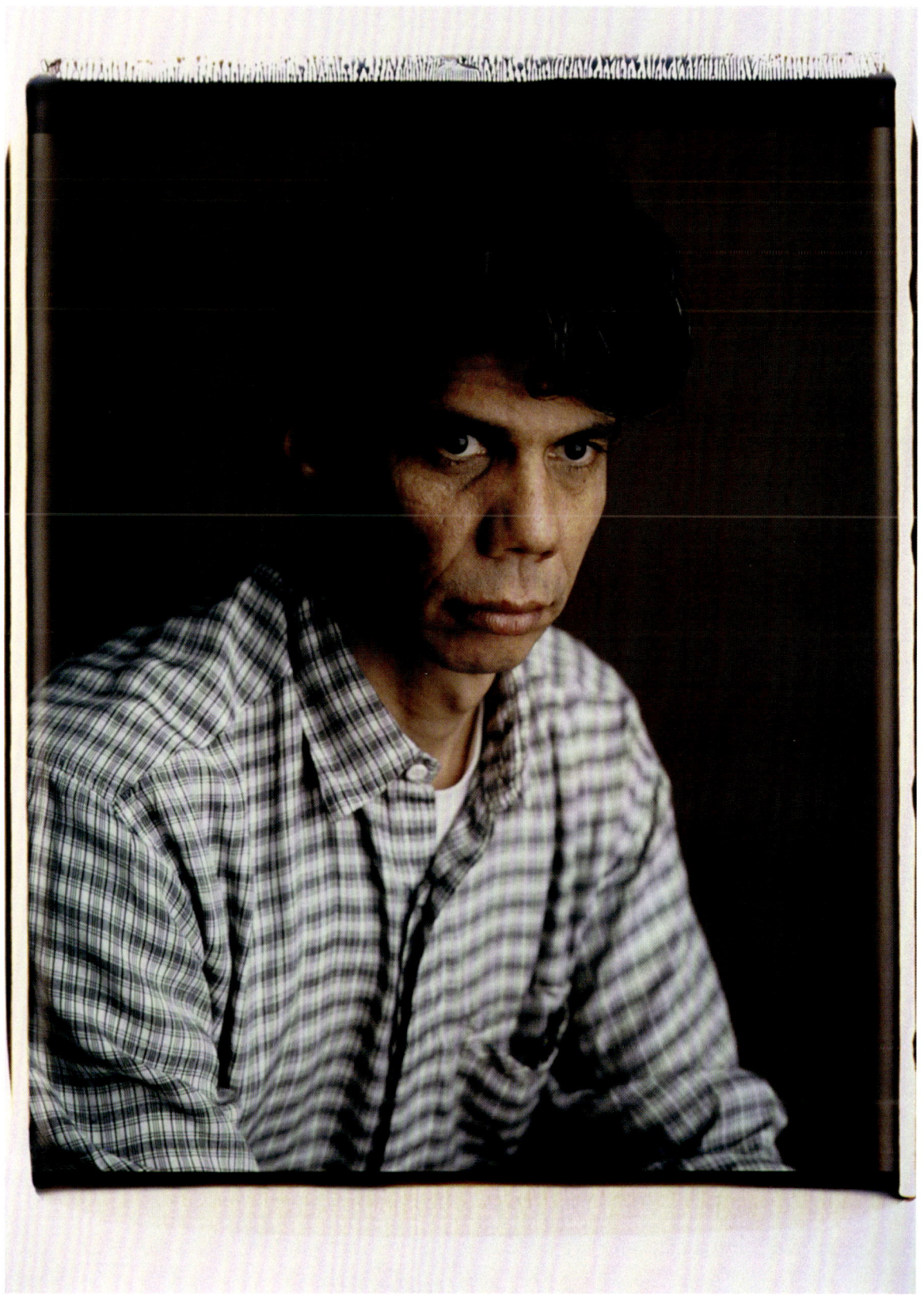

Dawoud Bey
Michael, New York, 1991

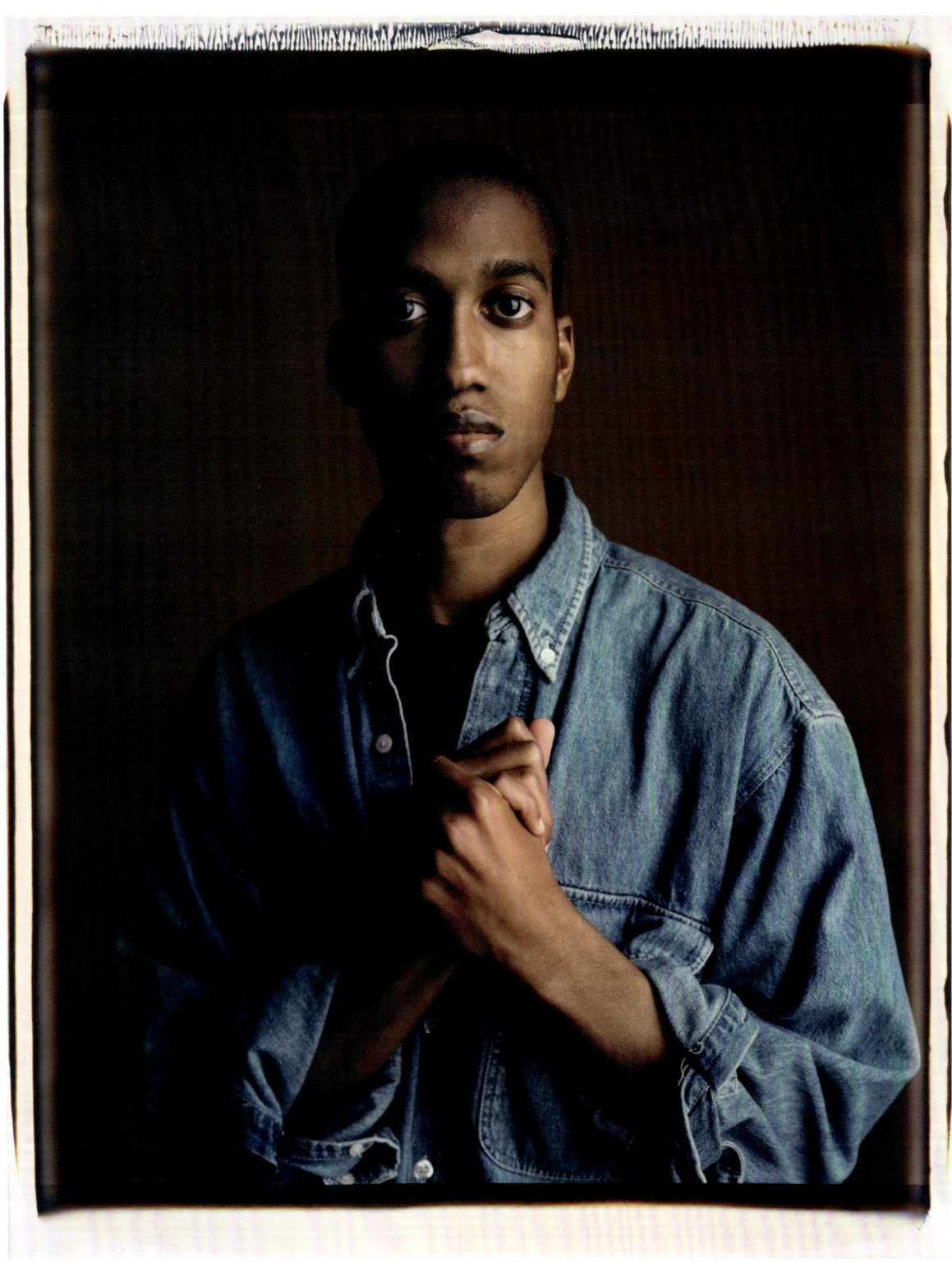

Dawoud Bey
Trajal, New York, 1991

Believing in Something

In the studio, I was not only confronted with the challenge of a new space, but also with how to direct my friends in the now-isolated environment. The first and most fundamental thing I worked toward was to shape the behavior of the subject to the frame. If the photograph was vertical, and the subject's arms were being cut off, I had to reposition them and reshape the pose. In doing this, I looked for fluidity in the form, ways to shape the body that were idiosyncratically expressive.

I still work this way today. I don't say, "Do this or that" because the person would look stiff, but sometimes I'll kind of perform what I want the person to do and I'll be doing it at the same time. Or I'll say, "do something else with your hands." I try to help them along with their own gesture. But it would never occur to me to say, "Clasp your hands together in front of your heart." That gesture is unique to the person.

Artificial light heightens the drama, as in a Caravaggio or Rembrandt painting This evocative quality of light is not just a practical device, but also an emotional tool, imbuing the subject with psychological weight. And with this added psychological weight, there is more concentrated focus on the smallest expressions and posing.

The real challenge is having to reinvent my idea almost every time, so that I don't make the same picture again and again.

Because, after all, how many gestures are available to the human body against a studio backdrop? Answering that question is part of what continues to motivate me. I take my cues from the person and try to locate some individually distinctive gesture or expression that speaks to the nature of who this person, in front of the camera, is.

I often ask myself why certain representations of people resonate so strongly. What is it that takes a two-dimensional picture from a mere representation to an actual experience? What has to happen for you to feel that you're not just looking at an object but having an encounter with another person?

I think in some fundamentally human way, you have to believe in the subject. What you're really trying to visualize in the picture is your belief that something is there. In the absence of that belief, the picture can become more descriptive rather than evocative.

I believe there is an interesting story to every person. The challenge is how to make that visible. Merely pointing the camera at a subject looking into the lens is not going to do it.

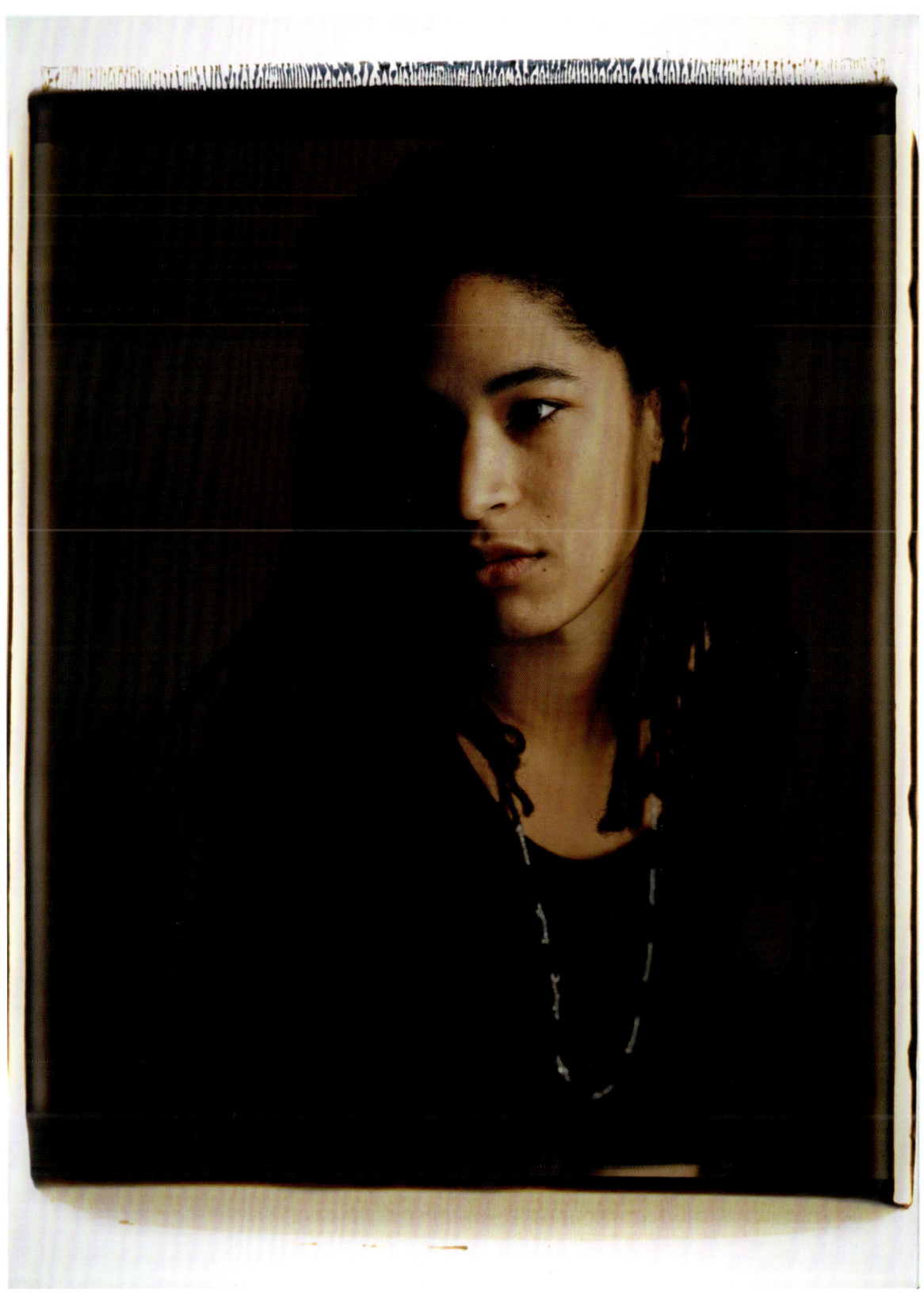

Dawoud Bey
Rebecca, New York, 1991

With a portrait, I'm authoring the experience of an individual with their participation, especially in the studio, where there's no other setting to inform the meaning. I'm the only one who knows what a person looks like in front of the camera. I'm looking for the way in which interior thoughts make themselves visible on the surface of a face at any given moment. Here it's that interiority—the sense of this man being lost in his own thoughts—that makes him appear a whole, living, breathing person. That's what makes the photograph believable. Because he looks comfortable, at ease, we believe—that's him; that's his behavior.

So how do you bring an aspect of interiority to the surface in the picture? For me, it's about making sure the camera isn't disruptive. In all of these pictures, there's a device between me and the subject, but when you look at these pictures, I don't want you to think of the camera. I want you to think of the subject, or perhaps think of yourself. As a photographer, you have to find a way to make the camera seemingly disappear so it's almost transparent. During the moment that I'm photographing, it's very quiet, an eerily quiet, contemplative space.

I often ask subjects to look away from the camera: "Just look away and relax." Turning their gaze away from the camera creates an even more private space, and the psychology of that reads differently than gazing at the camera. There's a self-consciousness in looking at the camera, but the photographer and the viewer are not being considered in moments of quiet introspection. These more interior moments are a retreat from the camera and, in some ways, a retreat from the world.

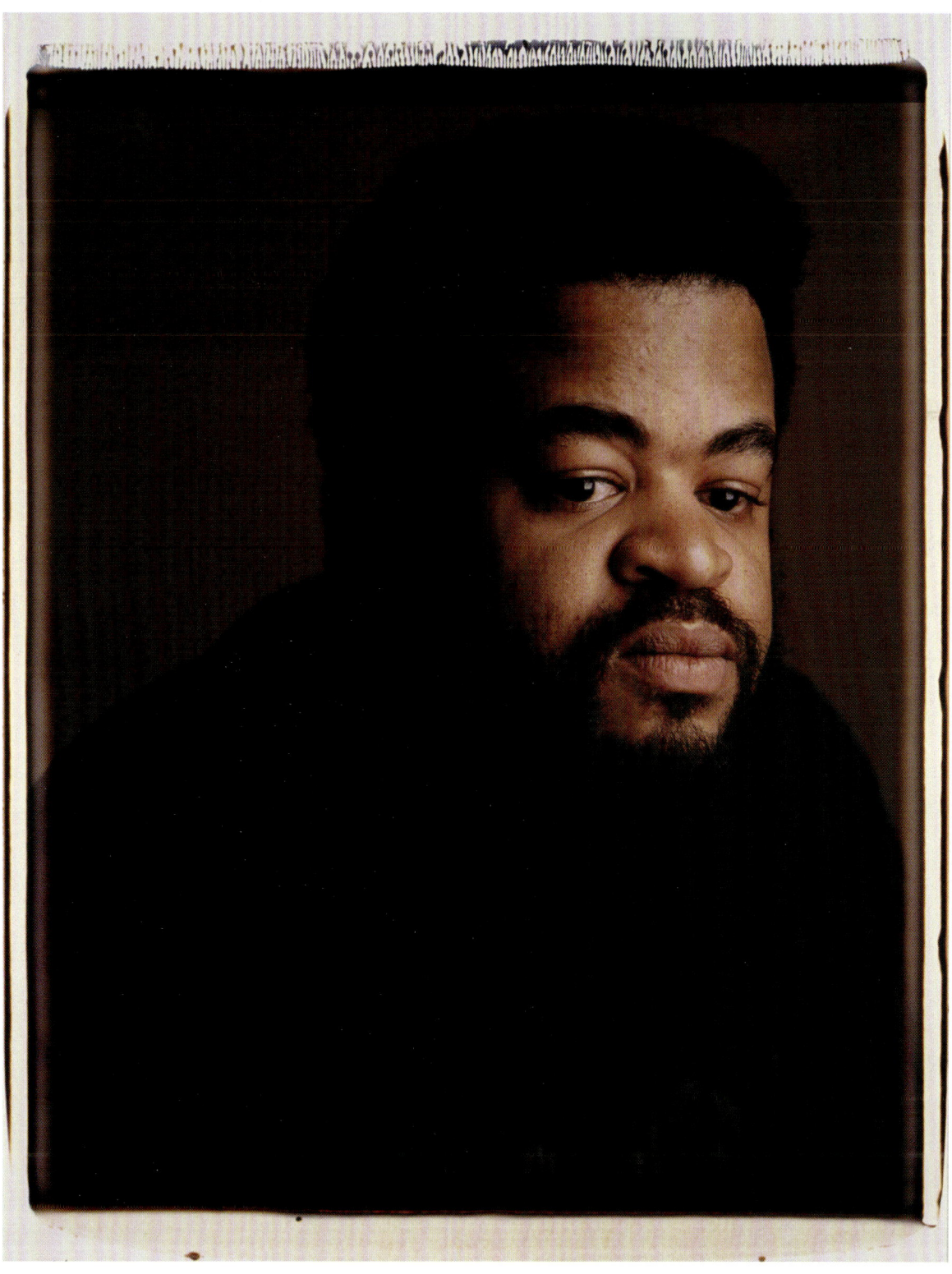

Dawoud Bey
Whitfield, New York, 1991

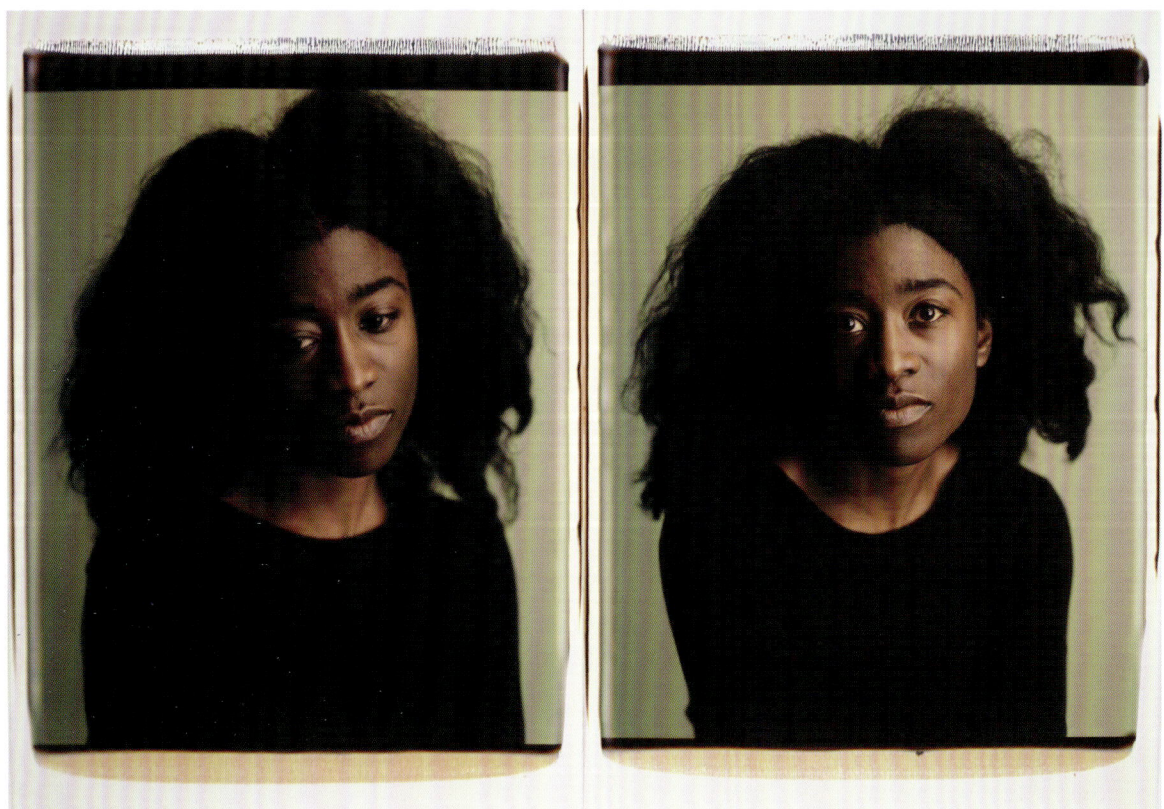

Where the Work Leads

In making portraits there are only two places the subject can look: at the camera or away from it.

I made a number of portraits with subjects directing their gaze toward the camera (and the viewer), and then others with the gaze directed away from the camera to signify an inwardly focused psychology. I wanted to create these public and private appearances in the context of the studio and then pair them for a more complex reading of a person. One day, as I was looking at all of the prints from a shoot pinned up on the wall, I realized I liked the way the images looked together. Rather than making a decision about which picture should exemplify a person, I decided to choose two to create a diptych—same space, different moments. Together, the pictures challenged the idea that photographic representations are a single moment that embodies the subject.

     Building this work, photograph by photograph, I continued to move past the conventions of photographic singularity. I also made multiple exposures and brought several moments into a single, whole image. Each frame depicts the passing of time, and the viewer has to move from one image to another. This is closer to how

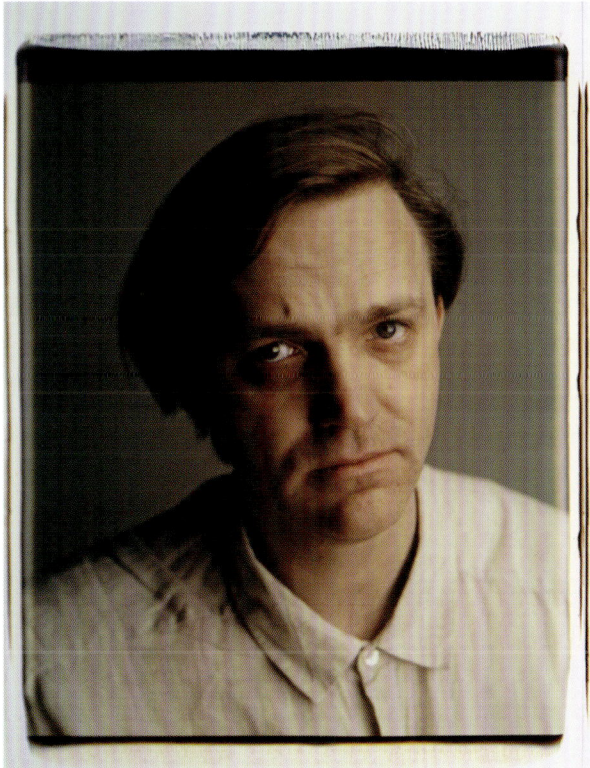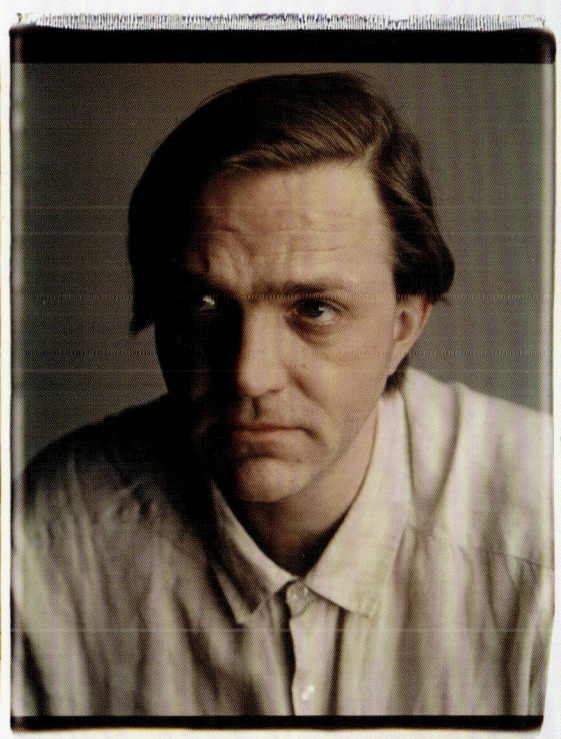

we really see things. You can't take in everything in one glance. You absorb a piece at a time and then construct the meaning and the whole in your mind.

But all of these strategies remain rooted in the subject. I've always been interested in the person, giving the ordinary people a place in the historical conversation. A viewer has to look deeply at the subject and engage if they're really going to *see* my work.

Above
Dawoud Bey
Rob, New York, 1992

Left
Dawoud Bey
Alva, New York, 1992

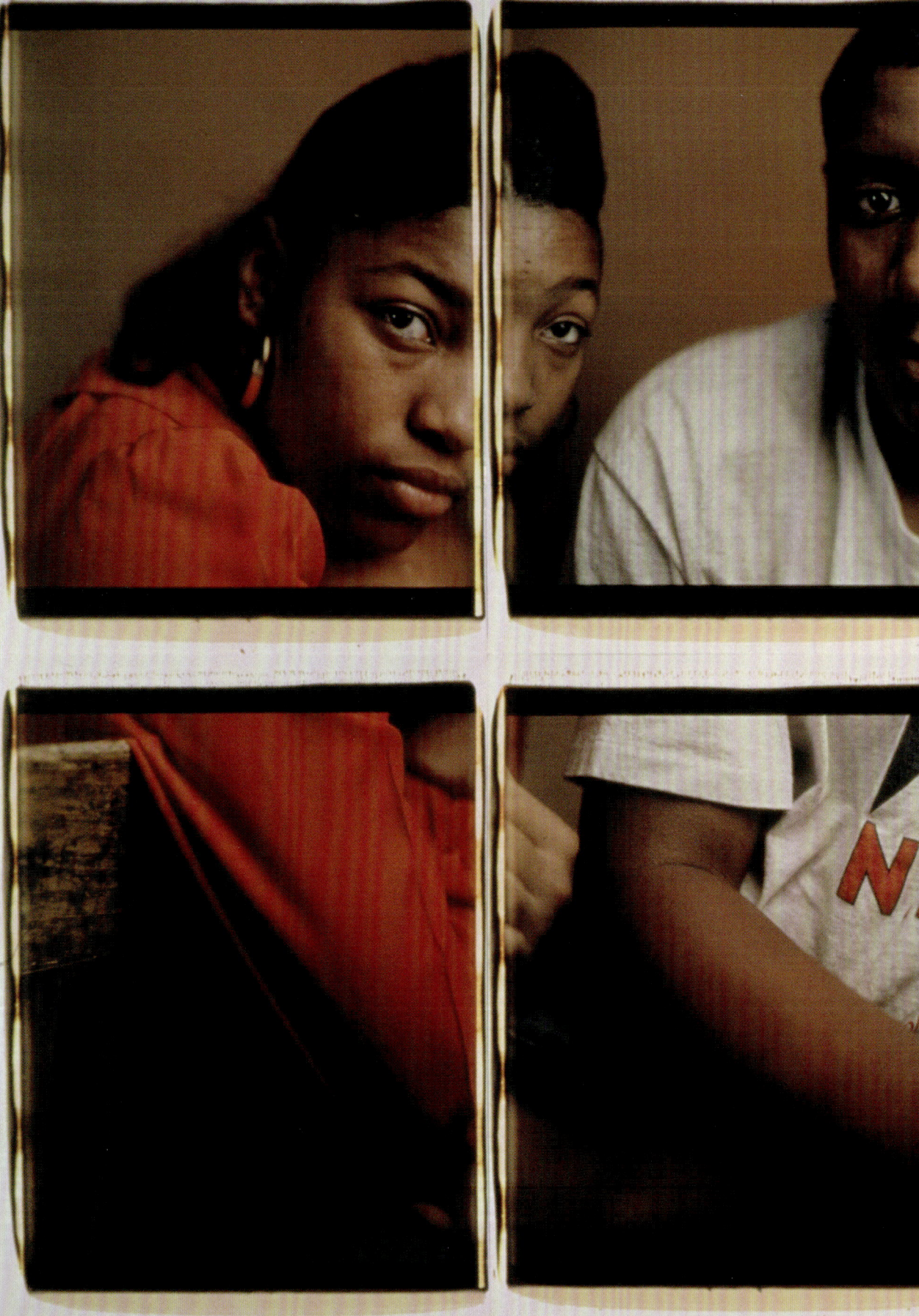

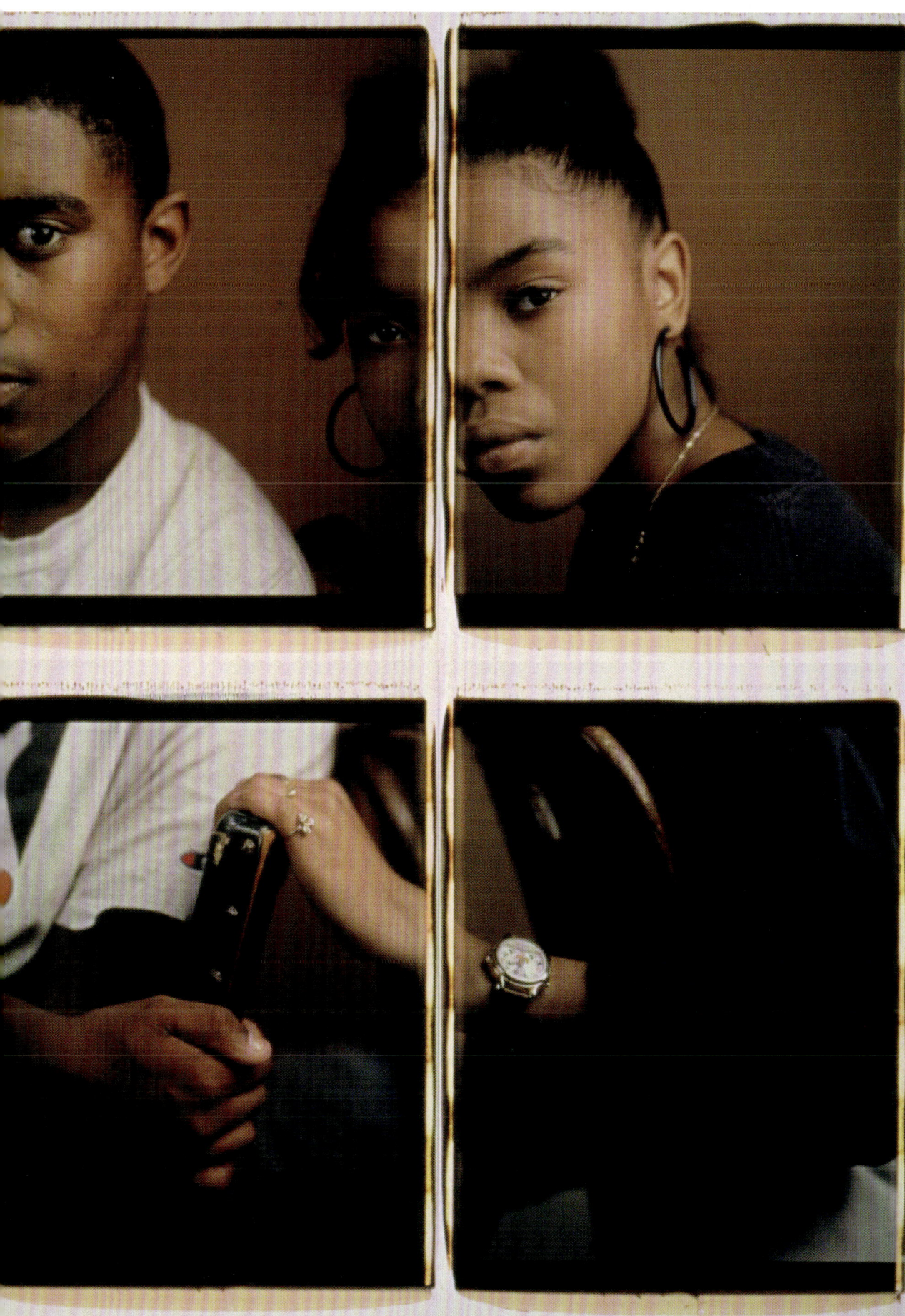

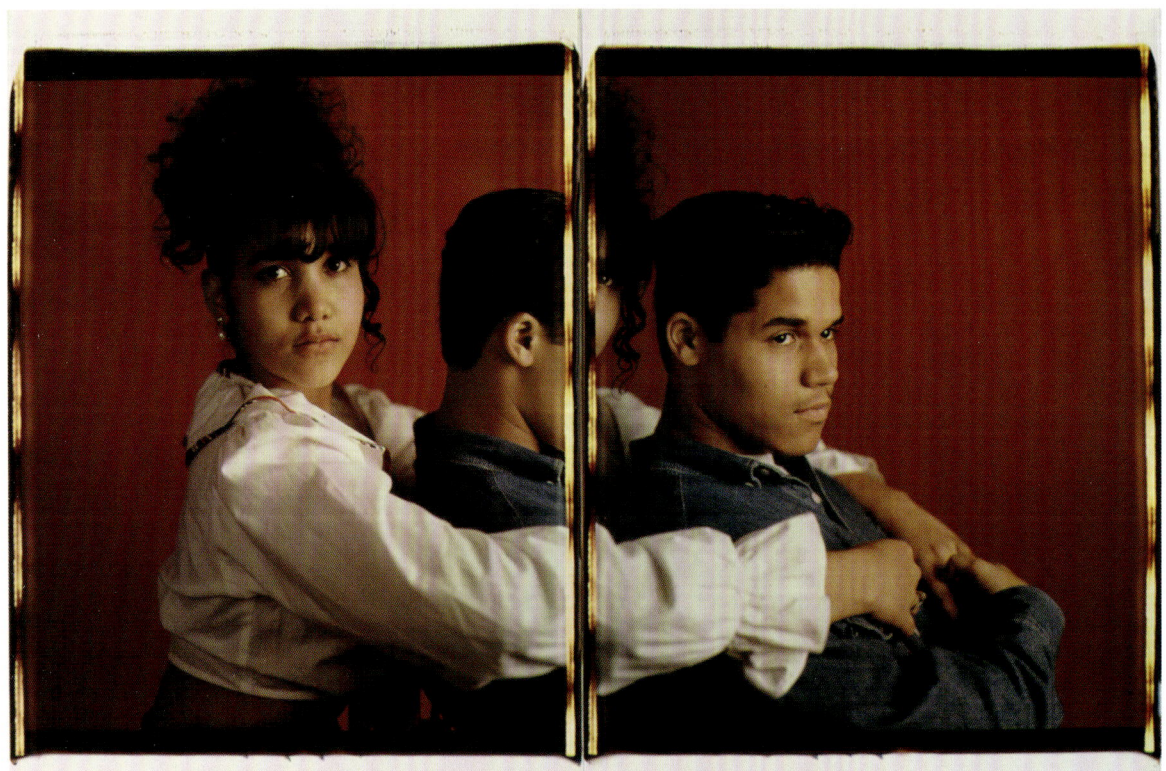

Where Art Is Made

Around the time I started working in the studio, I was invited to be an artist-in-residence for eight weeks at the Addison Gallery of American Art at Phillips Academy, which is a boarding school in Andover, Massachusetts. Artists are asked to engage in some way with the student population—that engagement is central to the program. When I was photographing with the 4-by-5 camera in the street, I made many photographs of young people, but the world of New England prep schools is very different from the world I grew up in. I was even more of an outsider there than I had been in other communities I had photographed. And I had my own preconceptions about what I would find. When I got there, I saw how those preconceived ideas turned out to be largely stereotypical. The population there was more diverse than I would have expected.

The residency also allowed me to think about how to make the private space of the studio more public. I began to make the photographs not only with students from Phillips Academy, but also with students from Lawrence High School, which was in an economically depressed town about fifteen minutes away. I devised a series of activities around my picture-making that brought the two student communities together.

Pages 76–77
Dawoud Bey
Toyia, Kelvin and Erica, Chicago, 1996

Above
Dawoud Bey
A Couple from Lawrence High,
Lawrence, Massachusetts, 1992

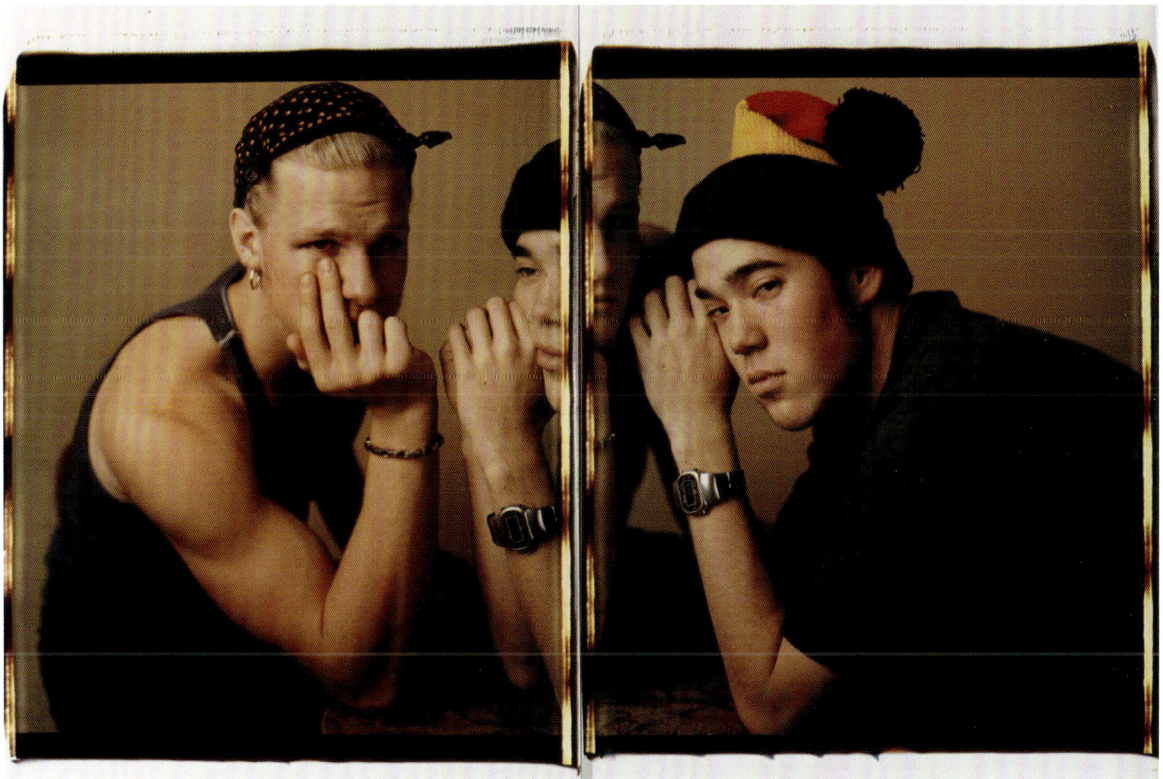

I set up a studio (with the help of Polaroid) in the Addison Gallery and had students come to the museum, not to see artworks, but to see portraits being made that would eventually hang in that museum. I wanted to open up the institutional space and flip this notion of the museum as a place where art is only shown by turning it into a space where art is *made*.

All of the pictures were made in a semi-public way. There were always young people standing around, watching me make these photographs. This context may not necessarily be evident in the pictures, but it has everything to do with how the photographs came into being and with the artistic process. It was important to the project to get young people into the equation of art-making and to provide them with access to the institutional space through my work as an artist.

Conceptual artist Sol LeWitt's work became increasingly important to me. He would come up with ideas for artwork and have others, often students, produce the final piece. It was a wonderfully generous gesture to make his art more participatory, to bring others in.

I went on to work with a wide range of institutions in a similar way after my time at the Addison Gallery, but that was the first time I began to think about how my work as an artist could be a catalyst to reorder an institution or a space, how it could extend beyond my ideas—into the larger social world, bringing communities together in conversation.

Dawoud Bey
Hillary and Taro,
Chicago, 1992

The Confidence to Not Know

I never know what the picture is going to be until I make it. You have the form—the rectangular space of the picture— as well as the framework of the project, but the rest is an improvisational activity that you enact within those fixed parameters.

After ten years, working with the same big camera for numerous different projects, I had worked through every conceivable idea I ever had about photographing in the studio. Though each project came with its own considerations, I was always trying to reinvent my own ideas about picture-making—going from individual pictures to diptychs to multiple-image pieces, moving around the subject and closer to the subject, bringing in more than one person.

There's a lot of experimentation and improvisation in picture-making, even in the controlled environment of the studio. Working with the small camera on the street early on and having a background in music served me well in being able to respond quickly in making the work. There's a confidence that one learns playing improvisational music. You understand what the form is, you understand what the parameters are, and then you jump in and keep playing until you're done.

You have to have the confidence to *not* know exactly what you're going to do but go forward anyway. This is especially true with the multiple-image pieces, because once you start, you can't stop until the whole thing is complete. You just have to keep going and hopefully you end up where you sense you're heading, with a piece that holds together.

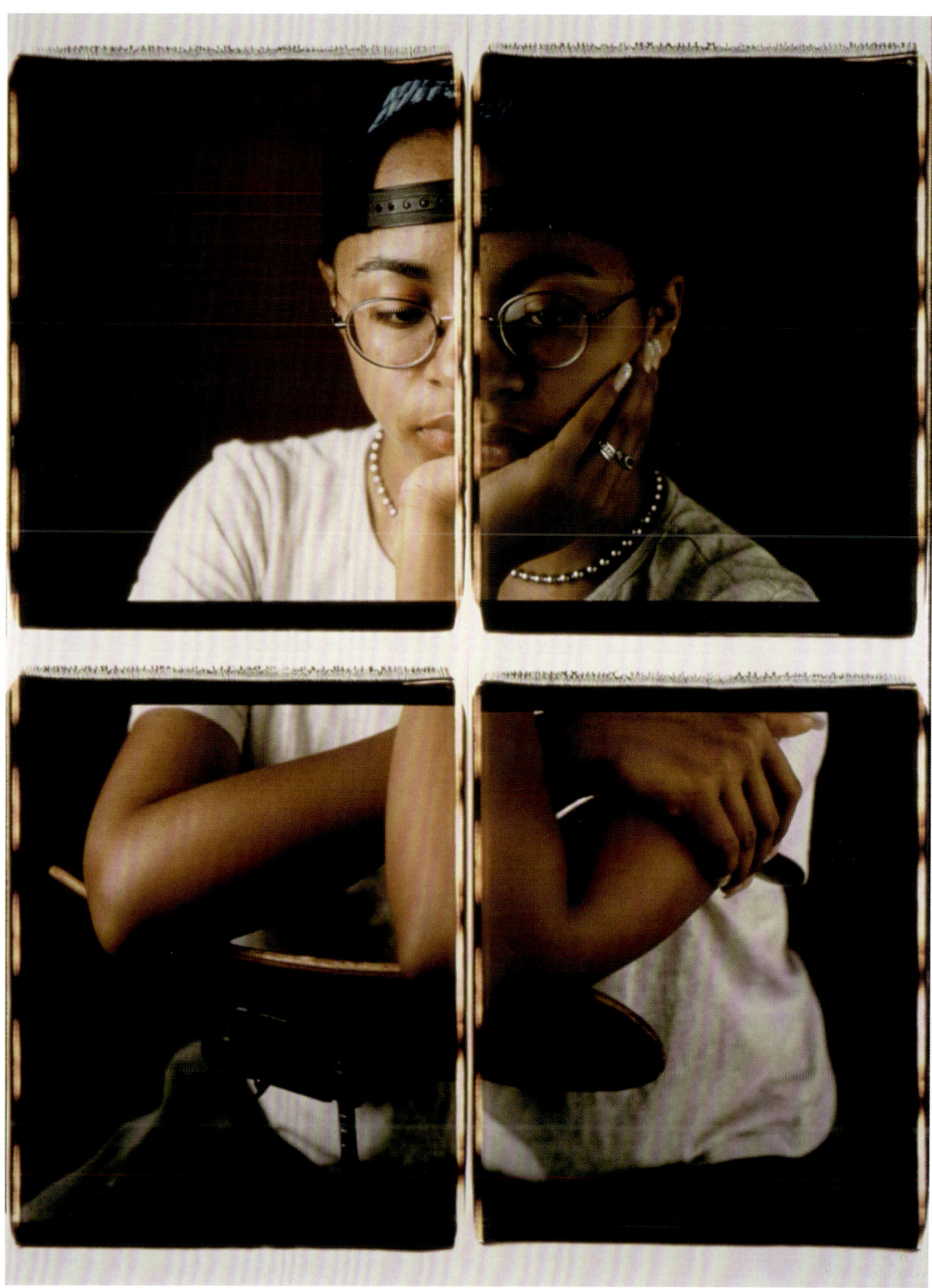

Dawoud Bey
Aurora, Andover,
Massachusetts, 1993

In making art, it's not that questions lead to answers—it's that the answers lead to the next questions, and you keep following the questions.

Once you've finished a project, how do you figure out what's next? For me, the next project is usually related to what I just completed. It comes from me asking a related set of questions and then responding to those questions with yet another group of photographs—answering them from a different vantage point or applying a different set of circumstances. You have to trust that guiding questions will come out of this process. This is why you have to always keep looking at and thinking about your own work in a responsive and self-critical way. The work has the ability to tell you what you need to know; it contains both the questions and the answers.

"I grew up in a lesbian family, and I met my dad when I was four years old. My mothers taught me to never judge or discriminate against others, and to look at them for who they really are. I think this point of view is something that is lacking in our world today. I feel so fortunate that I live in a place that I feel represents me perfectly. Every new day for me brings new and exciting adventure. I spend most of my time doing the typical things seventeen-year-olds do, but always find myself trying to take it to the next level, advancing my life as much as possible. Most people would say that I am mature for my age, that I don't act like I am seventeen. The only way I can explain this would be to say to them that I am very content with myself, and what I have accomplished thus far in my life, and I treat each day with the hope that it can be better than the previous." —Jordan

Dawoud Bey
Jordan, School of the Arts,
San Francisco, 2006

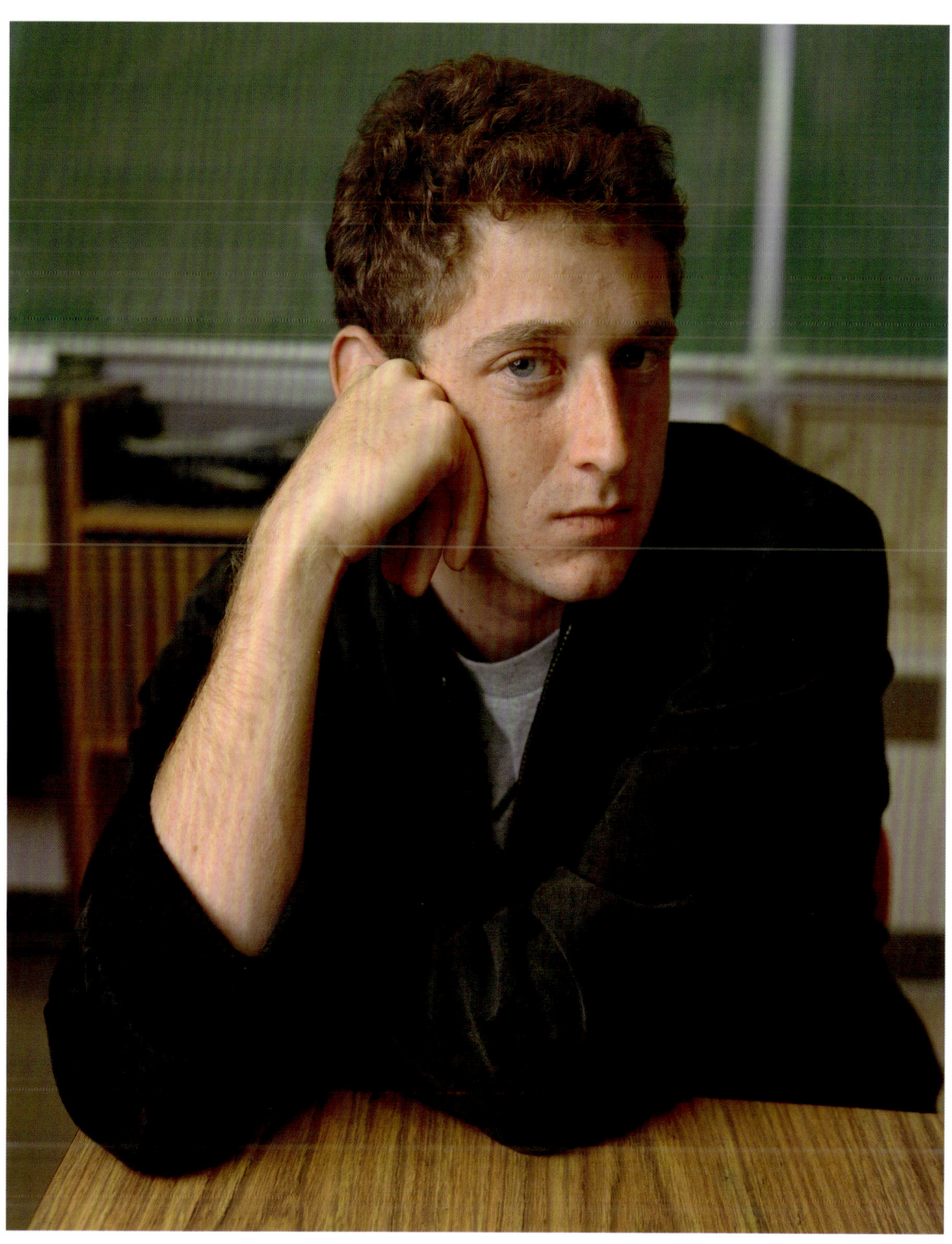

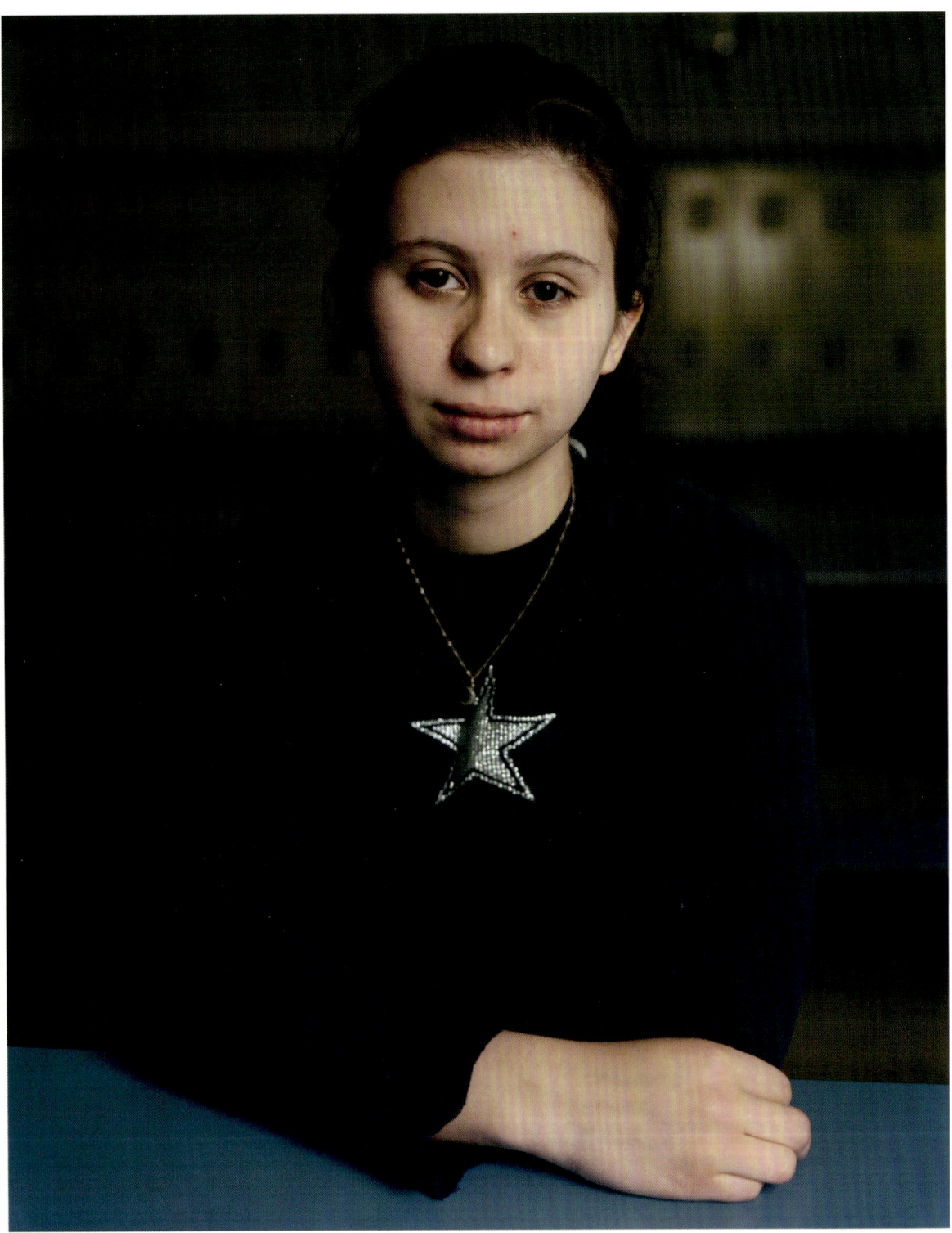

Translating Across Dimensions

Working with the large Polaroid camera was logistically complicated, which prompted me to return to making photographs in a natural environment, using the 4-by-5 camera, but this time bringing forward my knowledge of working with color material.

I continued to be interested in teenage subjects because I believe that this society, in spite of all its rhetoric, really doesn't care about young people as much it purports to. The culture tends to come *at* young people in ways that are useful for an agenda, representing teenagers as either socially problematic or considering them as engines for consumerism. They have been essentialized and stereotyped in just as many, though different, ways as black subjects—neither are depicted as having rich inner lives. I wanted to construct a representation of teenagers in opposition to that, coming to them as a way of finding out what they're really thinking about. And I wanted to make portraits across a broad range of educational cultures to create a more complex visualization of young people than the rather one-dimensional portrayal we see in popular culture.

When another residency opportunity arose, this time with the Smart Museum of Art in Chicago, I began a project called Class Pictures that brought together young people from three very different schools in Chicago: the University of Chicago Laboratory School, a private school; Kenwood Academy, a magnet school; and South Shore High School, a public high school. Over eight weeks, I photographed the students at each of their schools, and they engaged in a range of activities at the museum together. I worked with the students to curate an exhibition from portraits in the museum's collection that would be in conversation with my photographs of them.

From there, I went on to a residency at the Detroit Institute of Arts, and ultimately seven cities around the country. This extended the scale of the project, making it a kind of historical snapshot of the population of American youth at that time—much of it took place after 9/11, when questions of immigration were a flashpoint in the United States and the No Child Left Behind Act had passed to close achievement gaps in schools. Everybody was talking about young people.

"My dad's Iranian, and so, my dad didn't want to have me tell that I was Iranian in my college essay just because I think he might have felt that someone might read it and, you know, be biased against Iranians or something like that, I guess. He's a little sensitive about it sometimes, so, just because I'm his little girl and he doesn't want me to be hurt by anything. I didn't know whether or not to put it in 'cause, you know, when he first told me not to tell, it was sort of like, of course I'm going to tell! It's part of who I am! And then it's sort of, well, you know, maybe, I shouldn't. And then, I just ended up saying that he was foreign-born, "my father is foreign-born," or something like that. Like I'm not going to hide it from the world; it was just this college essay. I mean I wasn't happy about it at first, but then when I saw it from his point of view, I was like, okay." —Sarah

Dawoud Bey
*Sarah, University of Chicago
Laboratory School*, 2003

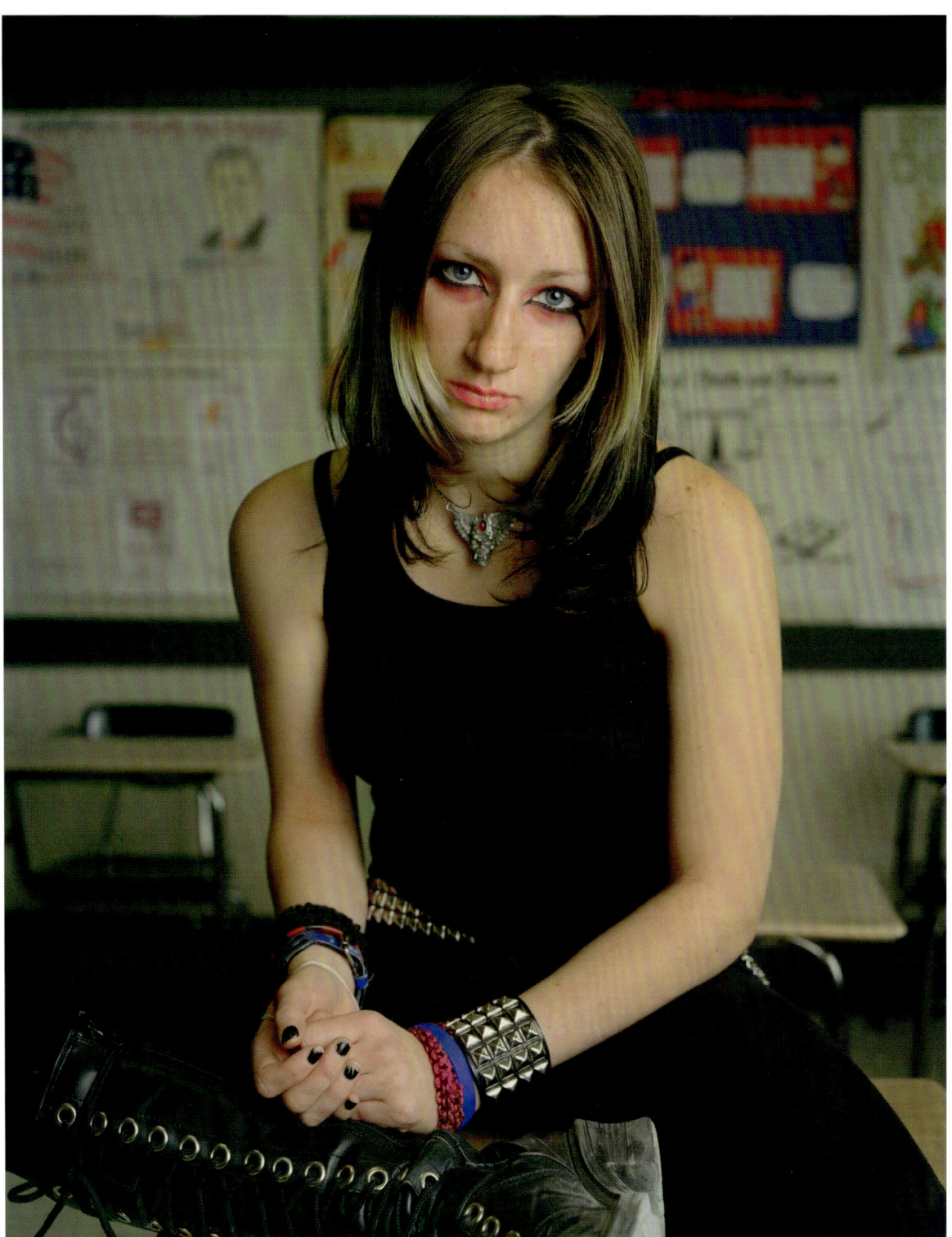

I've never really bought into this "passport" tendency in photography: the idea that your camera is a passport to go someplace more interesting than the place you are. What I want to do is to take a closer look at ordinary surroundings.

With Class Pictures, the photographs were always made in the classroom because that's where teenagers spend a significant amount of their time. I wanted that context to be present in the pictures but not to overwhelm the subject or dominate the portrait.

There's a conceptual framework that the work needs to exist inside of—the "what" or "why" (what it's about and why it needs to exist)—and then there's the "how." To create a photograph that lives up to the ideas, I have to bring everything I know formally, optically, and technically to the process. The three dimensions in front of me have to be translated into the two dimensions of the portrait, which conveys everything through the foreground, middle-ground, and background. I used a shallow depth of field to foreground the subject in such a way that you can see they're in a classroom, but you can't read the titles on the spines of the books. I'm also using the depth of field to push the subject into our space almost physically so that the picture is not just a two-dimensional object.

The lighting here directly relates to studio lighting, but I used a strobe through an umbrella, which gives the same kind of appearance as a soft box without being as physically imposing. I don't like too much paraphernalia. I wanted the light to look like window light even though there's nothing natural about it. It's light that doesn't look "lit."

I never knew in advance what the students were going to be wearing. I had to work quickly with color in the subject's clothes and color in the environment to create a unified space within the picture. I placed Sarah so that the red and blue of the bulletin board in the background echoes the red and blue of her bracelets and makeup: her black clothes play off the black horizontal borders and desks. I'm creating relationships between the environment and the subject to make sure there are no disruptions in the photograph, no dissonances, because harsh color combinations would distract from the subject. I take in all the details in the background and move the furniture around. I'm looking at all these things to make sense of them. This may look to a viewer like it happens intuitively, but I have to think very deliberately about it as the photographer.

"I may be different, but I take a silent comfort in my difference. My looks do not define who I am. I know that I am separate from the rest of my school because I look the way I do, not "normal." What is normal anyways? And who decides what is normal? My soul is not dark. I have dealt with pain and misfortunes. I have also had wonderful people and experiences in my life. Everything I go through, the good and the bad, makes me a better person, not just a better person but stronger too. My experiences define who I am. I'll tell you what I see when I look at myself. I see a young woman owning her individuality, being her own leader, not following the crowd, and I see a young woman who learns from everything around her. Now do I seem so strange?" —Sarah

Dawoud Bey
Sarah, Lawrence High School,
Lawrence, Massachusetts, 2005

87

What Lies Beyond

Photographs have inherent limitations. There are things they can't do; there are things they can't say.

As picture-makers, we try to load them up with as much narrative content and meaning as we can so that they begin to speak, but there's always a bigger world that lies outside of the frame. The photograph puts a frame around a small slice of time and speaks emblematically about the things outside the frame. The best that a photograph can do is to make a strong suggestion as to what lies beyond it.

I wanted to address that by bringing the actual voice of the subjects into my construct for the work. At the Smart Museum, in Chicago, I collaborated with two radio producers, Dan Collison and Elizabeth Meister, to bring the students' voices to the pictures. While I was photographing the students, Dan was interviewing them. In the final exhibition, a sound dome hung with each portrait so that when you stood in front of the photograph, you heard the voice of the student.

Bringing the subjects' literal voices into the presentation of the work made it all the more powerful. There was a girl who talked about her father's death—we didn't know it then, but she had not been able to open up about the death to her own family. Her mother came to the show, stood under the dome looking at the picture, and heard her daughter talk about the father's death for the first time. As you can imagine, the mother was in tears.

From this experience, I knew I wanted to continue bringing visual representations together with the voices of subjects. Their words provide context and give them more agency in the creative process. As I went to other schools, I began to ask students to write something about themselves, so that their texts and the photographs could be shown together. There was a risk that in moving to written texts that I would lose the intimate quality achieved with audio, but I said to myself, "Let me just see what happens."

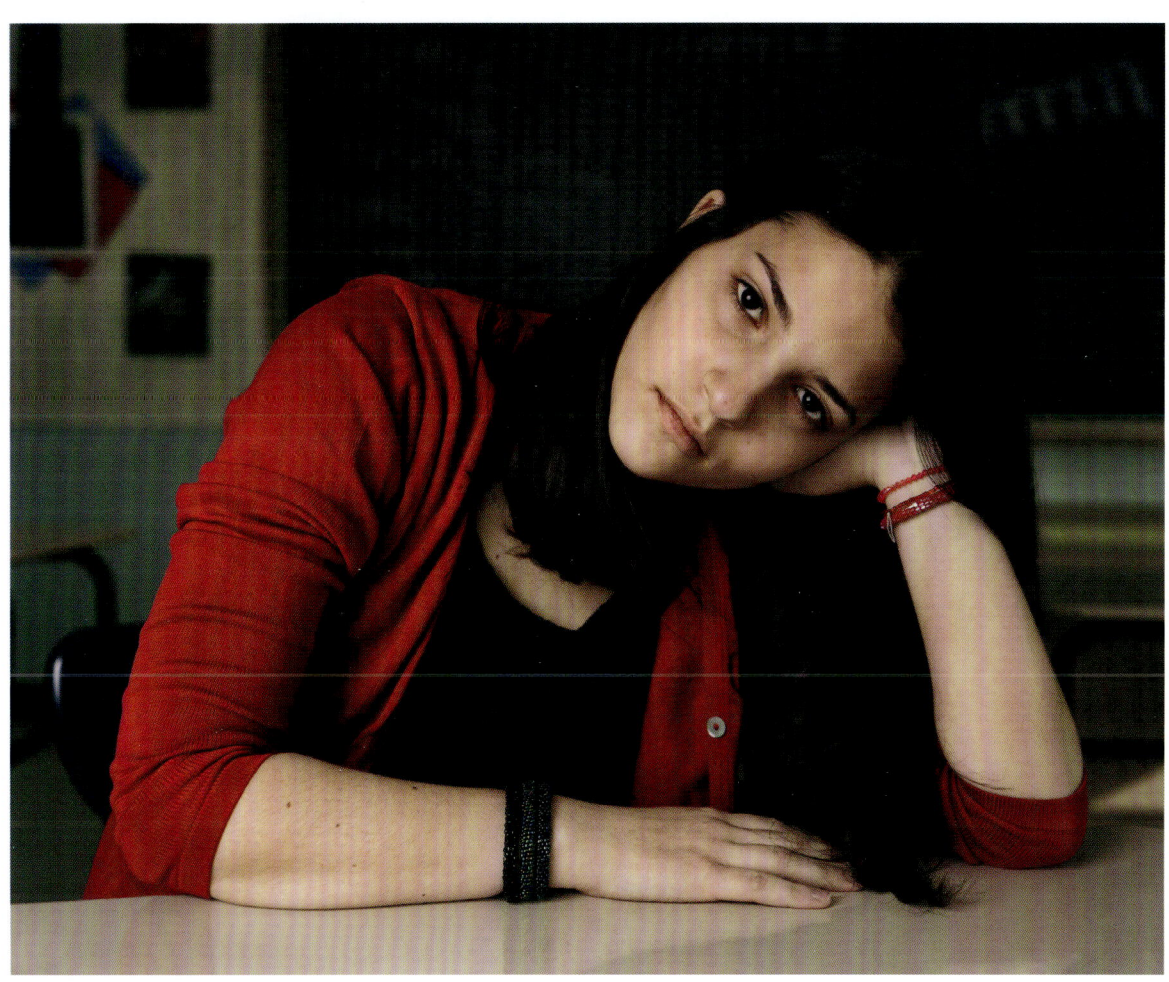

"My dad had been sick for a very long time. He was diagnosed with Lou Gehrig's disease when I was in, maybe, eighth grade, so I was about thirteen, and, over a period of about three years, he just disintegrated into basically nothing. He couldn't walk or talk or move or swallow for that matter, and then when I was sixteen, my sophomore year of high school, he died.

You just don't know what to do. Because you're just sort of stuck there, like, 'I can't do anything about what's happening right now,' and it's very painful. Because you sort of forget that there's life beyond that and, especially, that there was life before that because there was a period of time where it was, like, the disease and, like, the whole thing is engulfed and your memories are engulfed with all that sadness. And you try to get beyond that, but it's so hard. You have to move on with life, as hard as it is, and once you reach a sort of period where you can, and you can be happy again, it is very rewarding to be able to do that and to be able to pull yourself up again, and to be stronger maybe, to be able to do that." —Carolyn

Dawoud Bey
Carolyn, University of Chicago
Laboratory School, 2003

89

I feel most comfortable working in a space where I am, in some very real way, alone with the subject and using that intensified situation to make the photograph. Even with the Class Pictures work, where I'm working in the classroom, it's just me, the student, the camera, and the light. I like the heightened sense of attention that we are able bring to each other under those circumstances. There are no distractions.

When students came to be photographed, I gave each one a sheet of paper with a question. I tried to formulate a question that would provoke an introspective response. I came up with something along these lines: "Tell me something about yourself that you think describes you but that people might not know about you." This question presumes that there's more to tell than what's revealed in public encounters; it gets at the idea of a private self that is not on display. I allowed subjects to sit for as long as they needed to write something. When they finished, I would set the paper aside and we'd sit down to make a photograph.

I never read what they wrote before making the pictures, because I didn't want pictures to be responses to what they said, which would have been difficult at any rate. I wasn't looking to make a photograph that illustrated words as much as I was looking to make the fullest, most compelling representation of the person. I hoped that when the two elements—my visual voice and their literary voice— were brought together, they would add up to something more dimensional than text or photograph alone.

The stories they share come out of my curiosity and attention, my willing-ness to ask and to give them space. I think these qualities also make for a good portrait. The degree of profound self-reflection that these young people brought to the process was astounding. Their writings contain intimate revelations that go far beyond public ideas about young Americans.

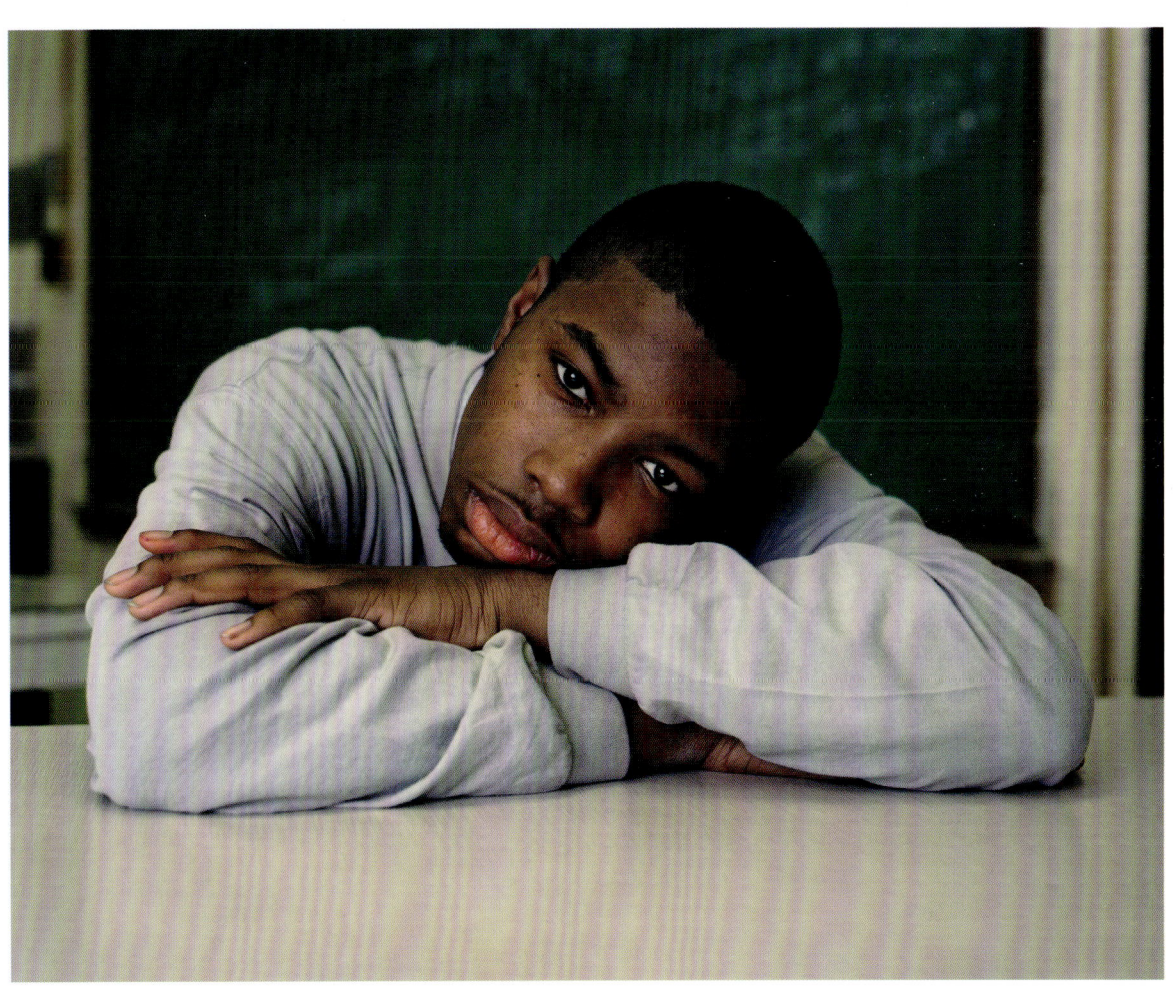

"If it wasn't for school, I don't know where I'd be. One of my friends just died recently, shot in the back of the head. He was walking down the street, him and a couple of friends of his. He was going back to meet his father 'cause his father was coming to pick him up. And then everybody started running; he was the only one who got hit by the bullet. At first I really couldn't believe it, 'cause, like, in the neighborhood we stay in, his whole family used to live around there, and he was like one of the main people that I actually spent time with. We used to go to the beach together, play basketball. He was a nice kid; all the adults in the neighborhood thought he was nice. It just makes me feel sad, you know, I wish I could have my friend back. That's why I try to keep my mind focused on other, positive stuff, such as school, making sure I do all my homework, so I can get the best grades I can get. I want to start my own record label, probably, and like open different types of stores and invest in . . . like, neighborhoods I've lived in and everything, have new buildings built so there'll be less homeless, get people up off the streets." —Kenneth

Dawoud Bey
Kenneth, Kenwood Academy,
Chicago, 2003

91

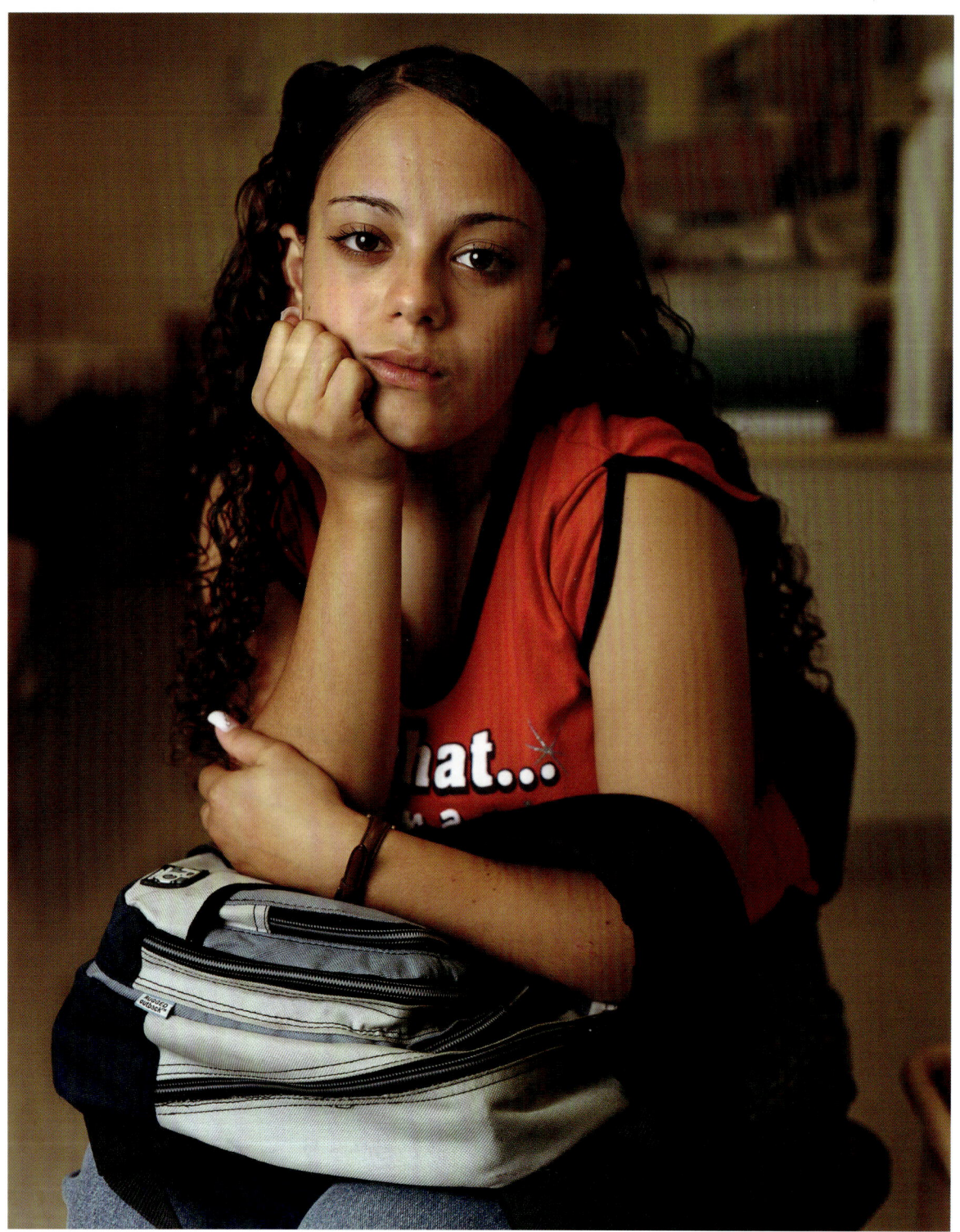

"I like to play with my baby. It's real fun to play with her, and I hope this
baby comes out, you know, healthy, and I hope that I can get out of
school and study. I want to be a professional doctor 'cause that's what
I want to do. I hope everybody remembers me, because I just started
in this school and everybody knows me, 'the little pregnant girl,' so,
I hope they remember me." —Odalys

Dawoud Bey
Odalys, Chadsey High School,
Detroit, 2003

Leading with the Pictures

Text does not make a photograph more interesting; it's either an interesting photograph or it's not.

The editing and selection process for this project was difficult because I had to deal not only with the quality of the photograph, but also with the quality and weight of the text. Sometimes the visual representation was stronger and had more nuance and drama than the text. Occasionally, the weight of the story was not quite matched by the photograph, and I edited those out. I believe the photograph has to have its own intrinsic level of interest as a visual object. For me, the initial editing process always begins with the photographs.

As I got further along in the project, I realized that the words and pictures would be even more powerful collected into a book, that the project's wide scope across America could reach a wider audience. It was the first time I conceptualized the work as something I wanted to be more broadly accessible. I wanted the stories to live in the book in a way that's much more permanent than online or in an exhibition.

While I had a strong feeling this could be a good book, I've never been one of those people who puts together a book dummy and shops it around. I just have too much work to do, and I figure at some point I'll get the project in front of the person who needs to see it. In this case, I got an email from Aperture after a curator had recommended my work to them. I put maybe twenty-five prints and corresponding texts from Class Pictures in a box and went to the meeting. They said, "We think this is something we'd like to publish. Would you be interested in working with us?" I said, "I don't see why not." That's how it happened.

If you persist and the work is good, career opportunities are bound to happen. At the same time, you do have to do some of what I call, "pressing all the buttons," reaching out to professionals to keep them updated on your work. It's kind of like getting on an elevator and hitting all of the buttons. This could mean different things, like going to all the portfolio reviews. Whatever, just press the buttons. If you press them, and three opportunities come up, that's probably as much as you can do. If only one comes up, do that one and then press all the buttons again. Even if the process is frustrating, a box of prints is better put to use in the office of an editor or a curator, who may or may not be looking at it, than under your bed.

A Catalyst for Conversation

I hope the work I do is deep and meaningful beyond the photographs. I am trying to create a conversation both about and with the human community.

Kevin, who is on the cover of *Class Pictures*, was the one student I wasn't able to give a print of his portrait. I always hoped that once the book was published and the exhibition started to travel, I would hear from him since he was so prominently featured on the cover and in a lot of the reviews. Sure enough, I did.

Some of my most moving experiences came not only in making these photographs, but also in hearing from the young people years later. Kevin went on to be a student at Emory University in Atlanta. He then completed a Fulbright in Morocco, where he did research on linguistic code-switching in the work of André Gide. He is an absolutely extraordinary young man. People might look at this picture and form an idea about who he must be based on his physical appearance—he comes from a very hardscrabble background in Detroit—but there's more to the story.

I intend this work—and all of my work—to be a catalyst for conversation and, in some large or small way, transform the viewer. They may encounter people who are not like them, but hopefully the portraits and writings fully humanize the subjects. The portraits provide an opportunity to have an intimate encounter with a stranger—someone who has had a different experience of the world—an encounter they probably wouldn't have if they met the person on the street. My hope is that viewers walk away with a different set of ideas, a different level of criticality, a different way of thinking about each other, and that they take that understanding out into the world with them. I believe that if you can make work that begins to transcend difference while locating a common humanity we all share, a radical reshaping of the world is possible, one person at a time. If I have any agenda, that's my agenda.

"When I was about six or seven my father died. This was either the worst or best thing that ever happened to me. In fact, now that I think about it, it was both. I don't remember much before the death of my father. For me it feels like that's when life as I know it really began. It's not like I was saddened by the event. I hardly knew my father. His memory only survives in my head because of three scenarios: the way his coarse mustache pricked my cheek when he kissed me, the short collect calls he made from the correctional facility, and the photos that my mother keeps under her bed. After his death my mother became a mere exoskeleton of her former self. With a dead father and a deeply depressed mother who basically stopped living, I had no choice but to take care of myself. There was no more time for childhood. I was all about business. Thanks to the death of my father I learned to value independence, hard work, and maturity. This is my blessing. Thanks to the death of my father I grew up much too fast and never learned how to ask anyone for help. I carry my own burdens . . . alone. This is my curse." —Kevin

Dawoud Bey
Kevin, Phillips Academy, Andover, Massachusetts, 2005

94

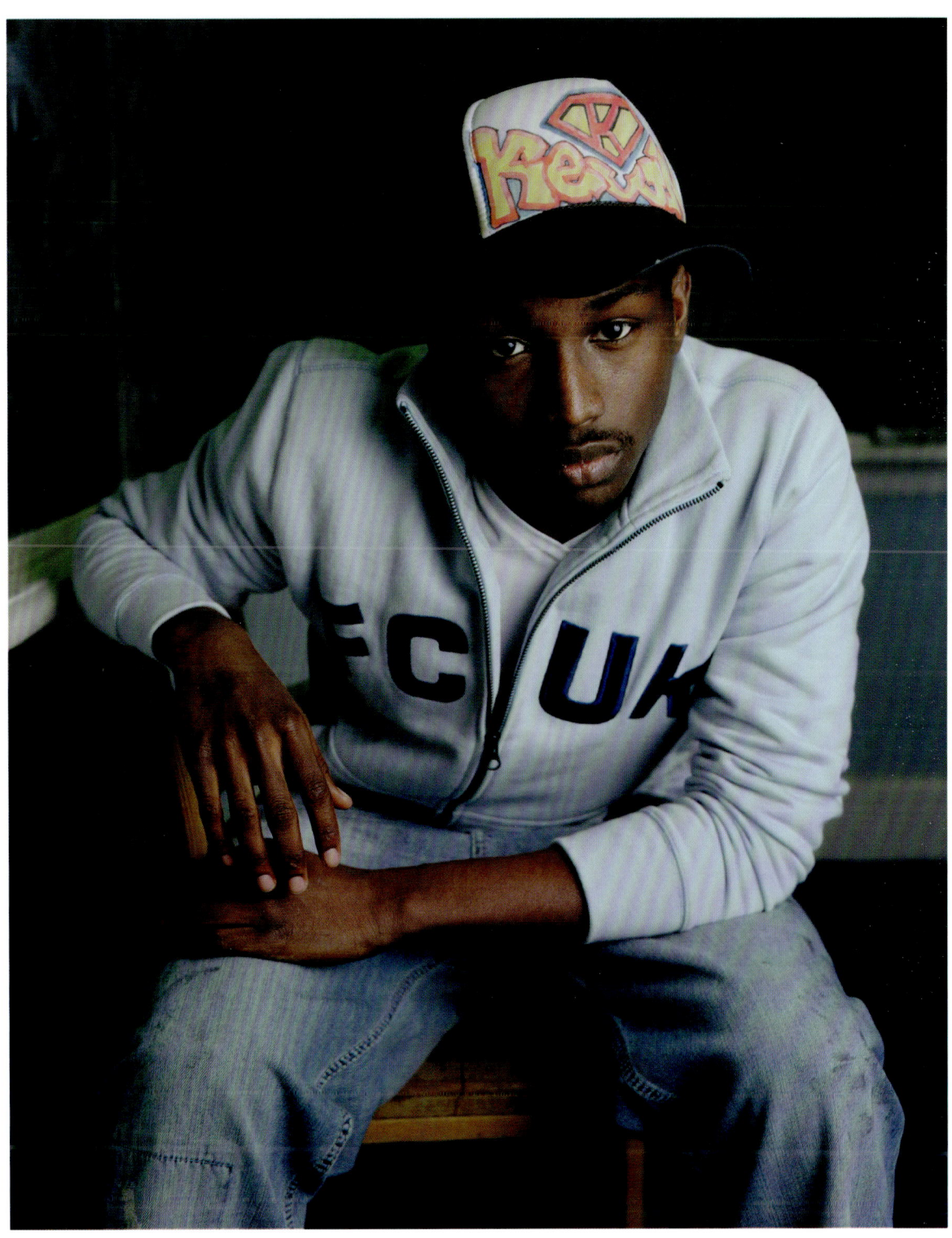

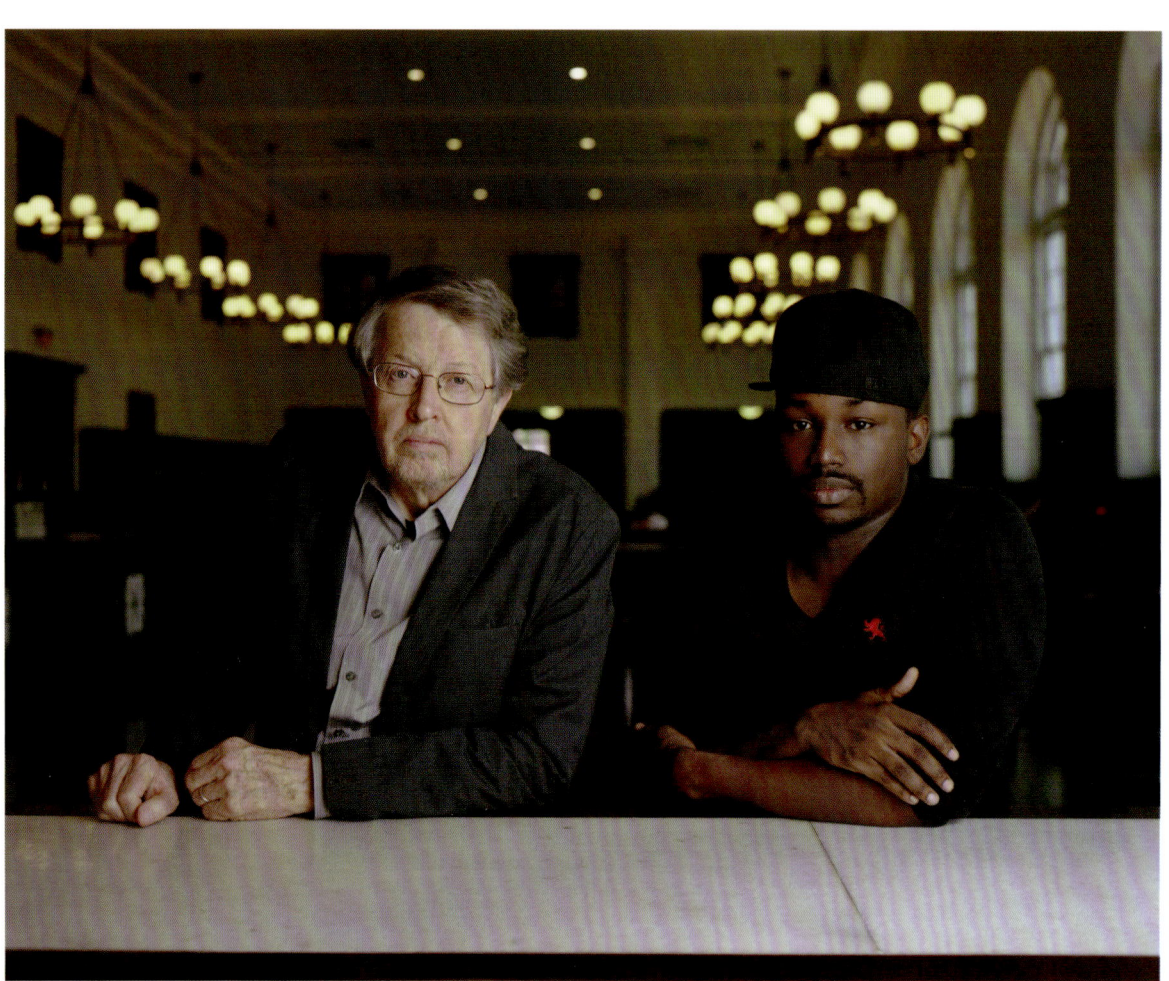

Dawoud Bey
Randall Burkett and Kevin Hatcher,
Atlanta, 2010

What Community Means

Who are we talking about when we talk about community? We tend to think about community in an overly simplistic way, as if communities are monolithic, when they are complex, socially engineered structures.

I wanted to interrogate the notion of community, how we are all related, and how we relate to one another—what it means to be together, and what it means to share common physical and social geography. I was invited by Emory University in Atlanta, and then by other campuses in the United States to visualize this complex notion of community through the Strangers/Community project. I brought people together who were from different social groups on campus and didn't know each other and had them sit together for a portrait. I cast all the subjects through campus outreach.

      The work that I'd done in the past had been primarily with individuals, getting at a sense of community through a series of individual pictures. In this project, I photographed two people together for each picture. They form a new community momentarily in front of the camera, and by extension, in the larger world. I wanted them to navigate the encounter in their own way. They're not in the dark about the project. They know that part of the picture is negotiating how they're each different *and* the same. They look very different but there's commonality, a shared community. They had to make a decision about how to present themselves to the camera with this in mind. Often one person ended up mimicking the pose of the other. It became a way of silently bonding with another human being and channeling that person's behavior.

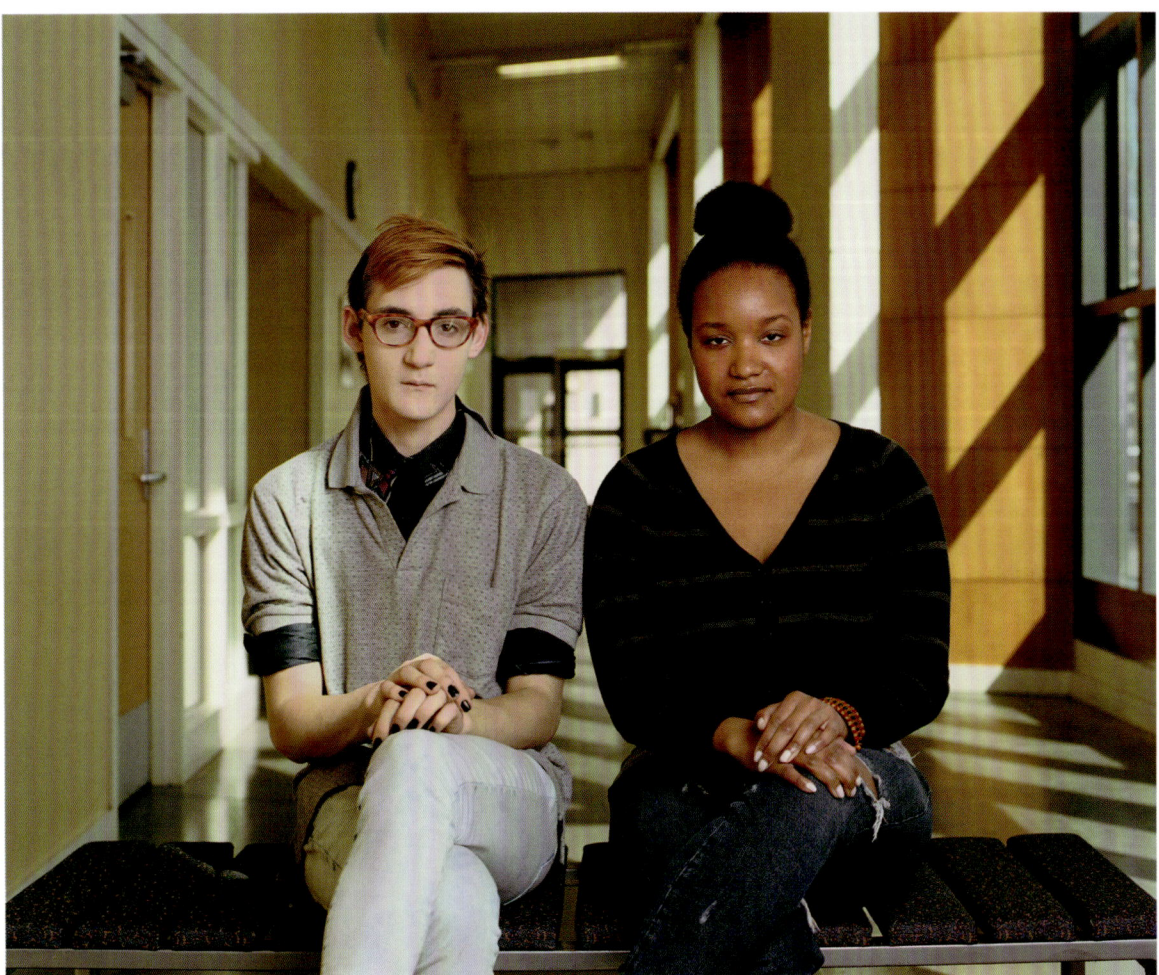

I wanted the narrative of a communal space, in this case a college campus, to be the setting, and inform the idea of community. Each person brings their own personhood to the moment and the place has its own meaning—the way it wraps around the narrative of the two individual subjects meeting in the photograph. These three narrative elements—of the individuals, the space, and the community—have to come together coherently to form a single piece.

I made snapshots of the subjects when they volunteered and then worked out the basic configurations beforehand. I had some sense of what might happen in the picture because I had created the pairings, but both people had to show up in order for what might happen to actually happen.

You're seeing pictures from the finished project, but each of these images was once a work in progress. I woke up some days ready to let the project go, and on other days, committed to figuring out how to move it forward. I needed

Dawoud Bey
Nicholas Karaberis and Monica Melton,
Tacoma, Washington, 2013

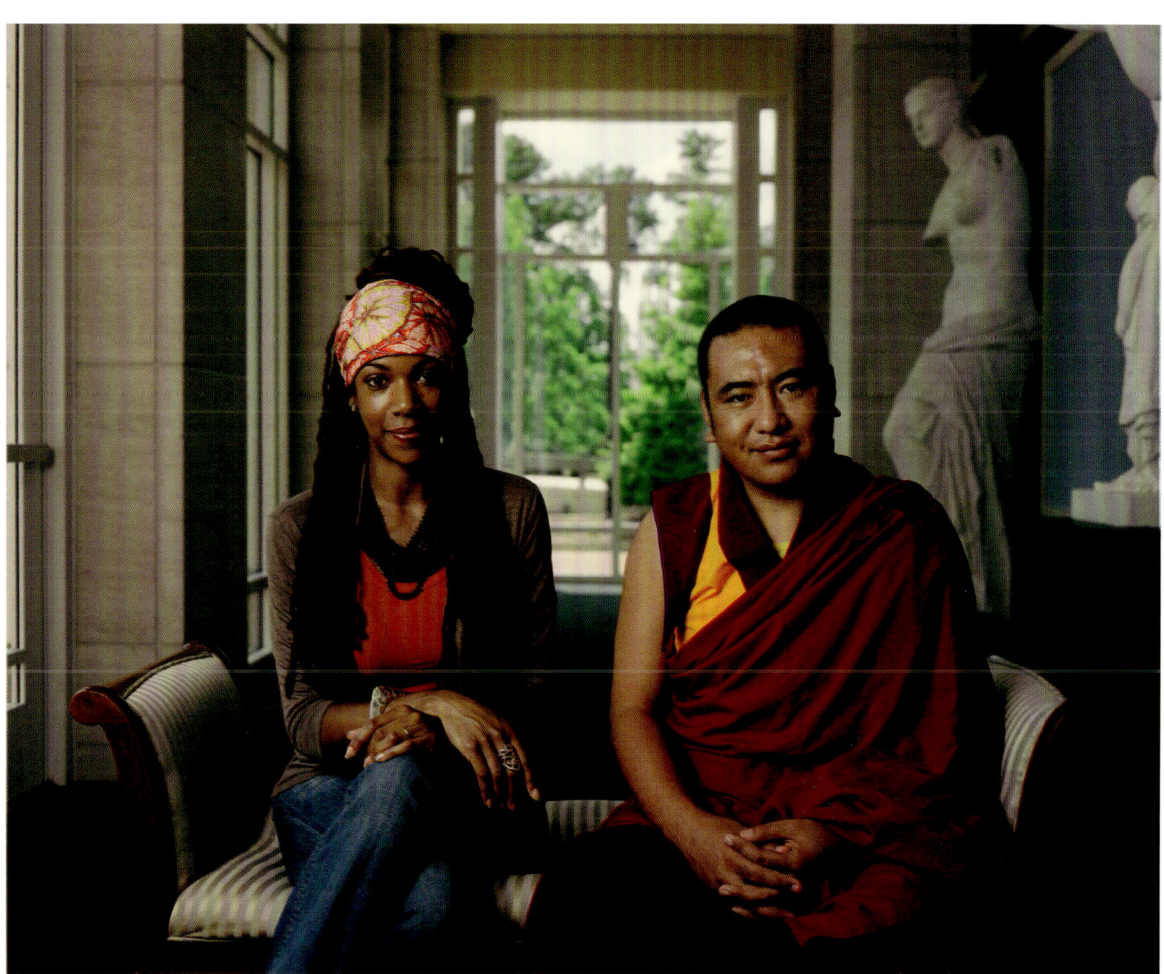

both people to buy into what I was trying to do and to be fully and comfortably present. Sometimes people just couldn't do that; it doesn't always work out. You still make the best picture you can and thank them for showing up. But not every picture is going to work. The important thing is to keep working. Don't trip over the ones that don't work; instead hope the next one is better and build off your successful images.

Dawoud Bey
Kali-Ahset Amen and Geshe
Ngawang Phende,
Atlanta, 2010

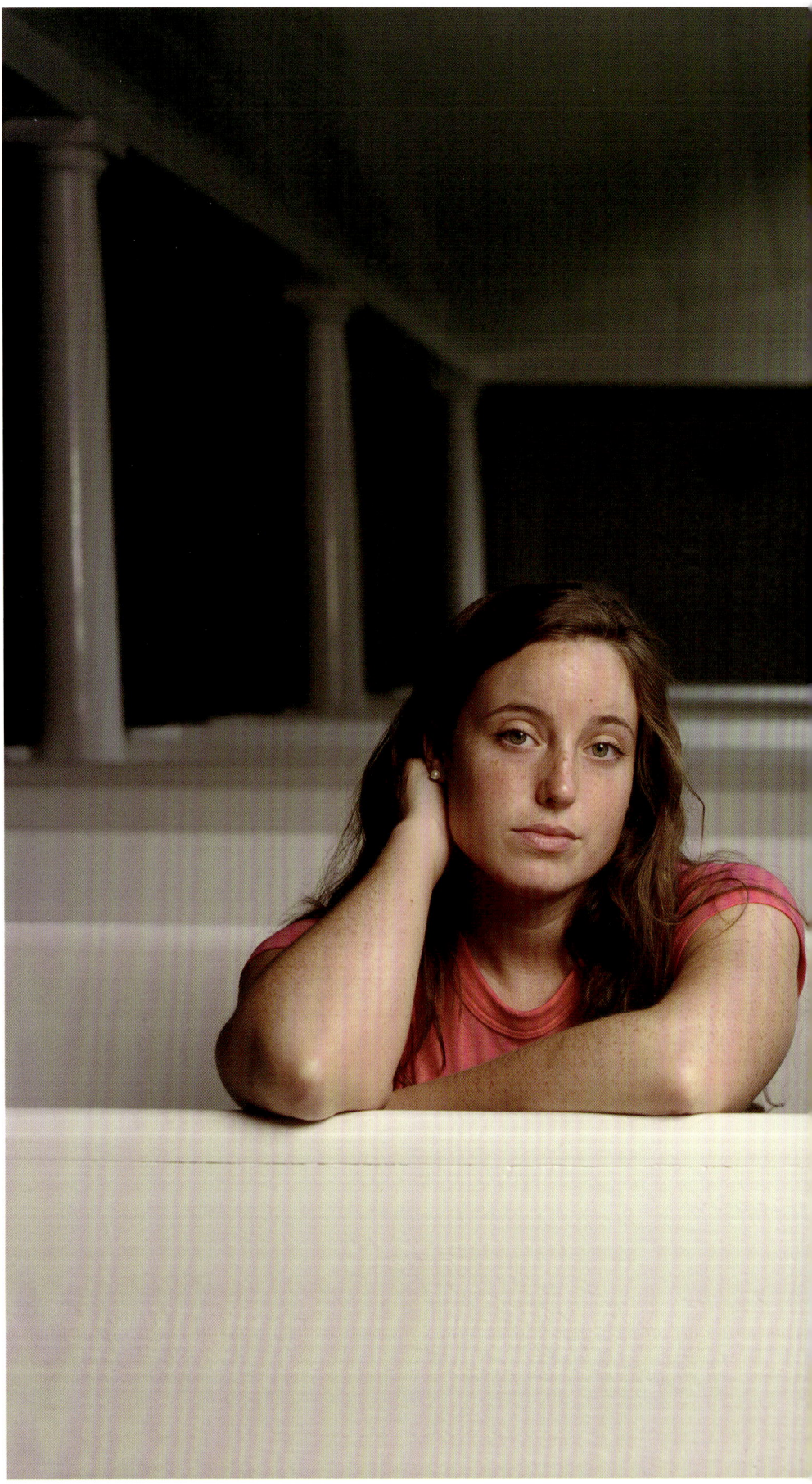

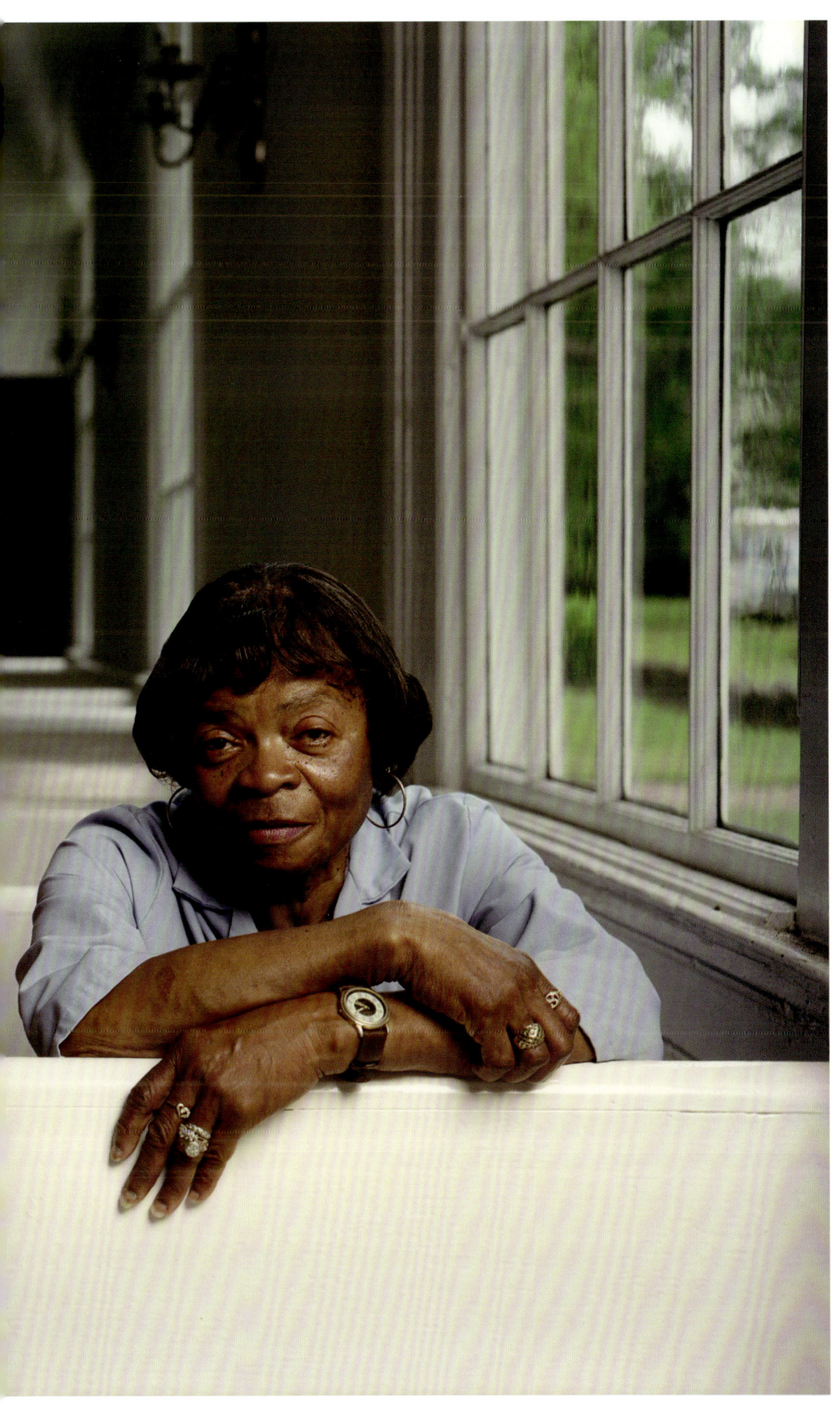

For the most part, these pictures are of adults. One of the curious things I discovered during the project is that adults have a high degree of self-consciousness. You would think that would be more true of teenagers, but I can testify that adults have a lot more invested in constructing an identity, and that their identity has a lot to do with their job or role in the community.

In some cases, bringing people together revealed social tensions that had gone unspoken. When I was working at Emory, one of the subjects was an African American man—I think he was the provost, certainly a college administrator—and the other subject was a white man on the maintenance staff. I wanted all the ideas embedded in whiteness and privilege to be present in the picture when I brought them together. The maintenance man was quite nervous beforehand; he asked me, "How do I address him? Do I call him Mr. Thompson or Provost Thompson?" I said, "You can just call him Bill. That's what I'm going to call him." The camera laid bare some of those tensions.

Ultimately, viewers determine, through their own subjectivity, what community means to them in the pictures. They can hopefully examine some of the preconceived notions they bring to the pictures and the assumptions operating behind those ideas. What is community? Is it possible to transcend roles? What does it mean to come together in a larger sense; is it even possible? I'm trying to raise questions with the pictures and the people in them. For me, there are always question marks. In this moment—this highly polarized time we're living in, where forces seek to divide people more than bring them together—it's even more unclear. It's possible that we can't be together; and then what? We're all struggling with how to answer these questions.

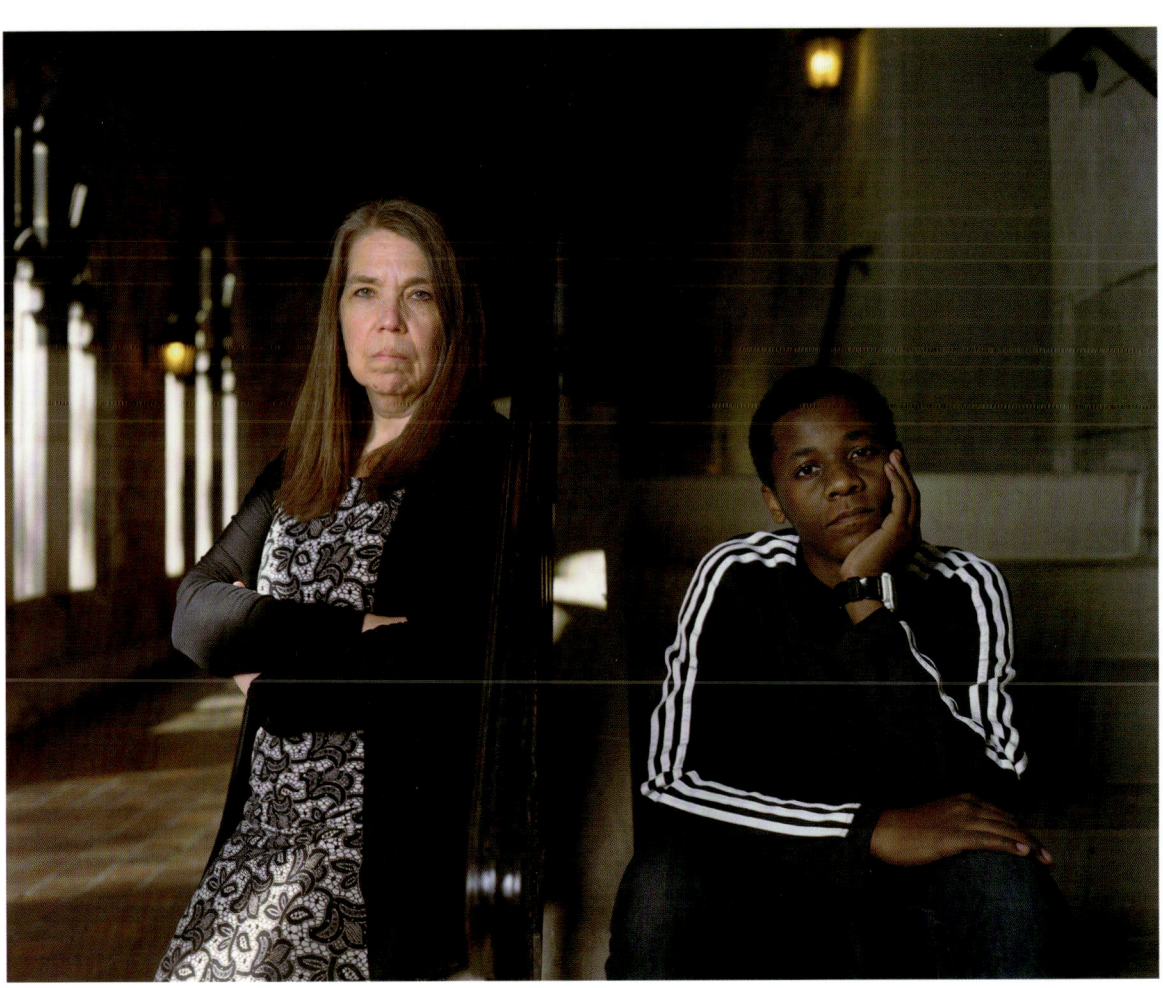

Dawoud Bey
Kathy Anderson and Jarrett Lampley,
Hyde Park, Chicago, 2012

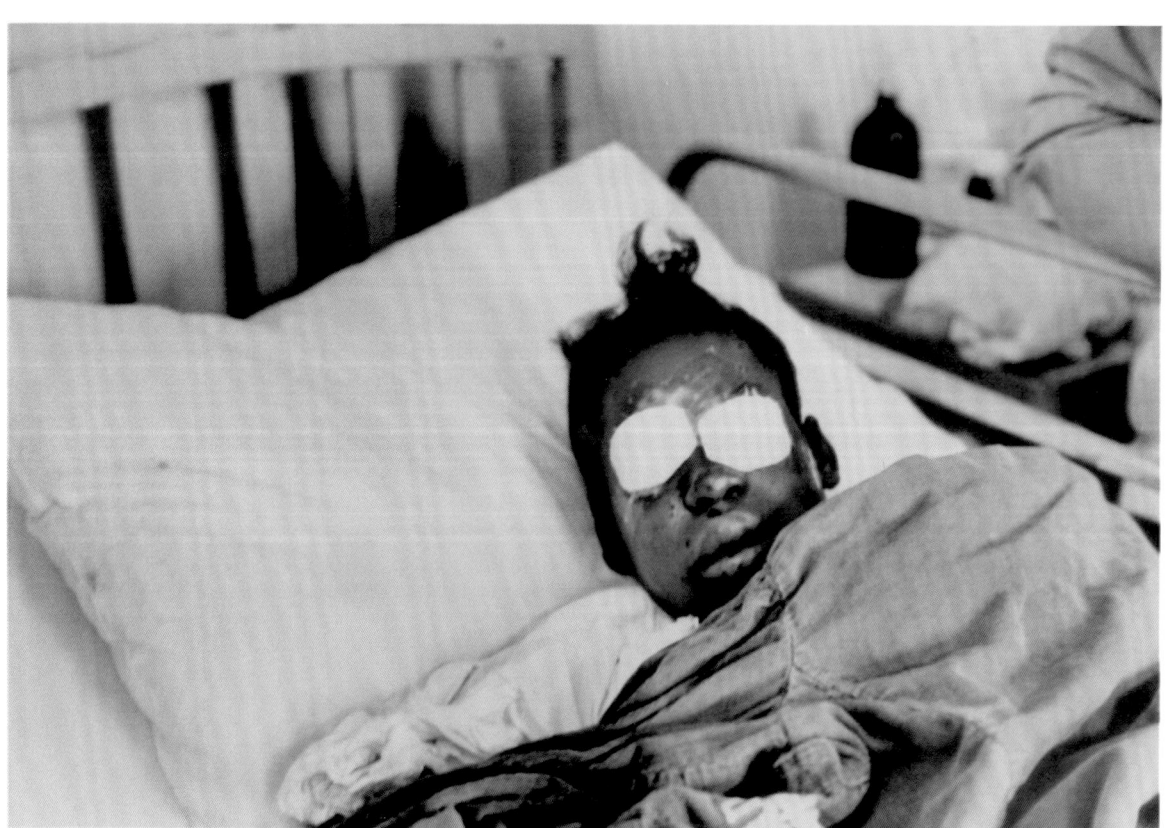

Frank Dandridge
Hospitalized bomb blast victim Sarah Jean Collins, 12, blinded
by dynamite explosion set off in basement of 16th Street
Baptist Church. The blast killed her sister and three other girls
as their Sunday school class was ending, September 15, 1963

The World After

I had heard the expression "bolt upright" before, but I had never experienced it until one morning when I woke up with a start, remembering a photograph I had seen when I was eleven years old. It was in a book called *The Movement: Documentary of a Struggle for Equality* by Lorraine Hansberry. In 1964, my parents had gone to hear James Baldwin speak in our church in Queens, where the book was sold to fundraise for the Student Nonviolent Coordinating Committee. They brought the book home without saying too much about it: they just left it somewhere I would see it. The book had photographs of the civil rights movement in it, as well as lynching and other violent images that really shook my secure place in the world as a young black boy in Queens, New York.

One picture stood out to me in particular, that of Sarah Jean Collins in her hospital bed. She was one of the survivors of the KKK bombing of the 16th Street Baptist Church in Birmingham, Alabama, on September 15, 1963. Her sister and three other girls had been killed in the blast. She was wounded and partially blinded.

That photograph seared itself into my psyche. There was the world before the photograph and the world after. In a very deep but unacknowledged way I must have known that I was pretty much the same age as the girl in the photograph.

I had been carrying around the trauma in that photograph for almost fifty years. I don't remember exactly what shook it loose and brought it to the forefront of my mind, but I started thinking about that photograph again, and thinking about that moment in history. I told myself that I needed to go to Birmingham, that I needed to both confront and engage that history.

But all I knew of Birmingham was from 1963, from photographs and civil rights history. I had no relationship to the place. I needed to supplement, if not supplant, this image that I had been carrying around all of these years with the Birmingham of the present. So, I went to Birmingham with the idea of making some work there but had absolutely no idea what kind of work I would make.

The Past in the Present

There was just too much that I didn't know to go to Birmingham and make work based on what I did know.

I was working on other projects but made several trips over a period of six years to steep myself in the history and absorb the experience of the place. I started spending time at the Birmingham Civil Rights Institute, where they have an extensive archive of material from the civil rights era, including newspapers from the day after the bombing. The time I spent learning was as much a part of the process as making the work.

During my research, I learned that not only had the four girls been killed in the bombing of the 16th Street Church, but also that two boys had been killed in the aftermath of the violence that began that morning. One of them, Johnny Robinson, was shot in the back by a police officer in downtown Birmingham; the officer said he saw the boy throwing rocks at a car with white passengers. The other boy, Virgil Ware, was killed by two sixteen-year-old white teenagers. After the bombing, the KKK and the White Citizens Council called a rally to celebrate; the two teenagers left the rally looking to add to the mayhem of that day. They spotted the Ware brothers and shot Virgil Ware right off the handlebars of his brother's bicycle. For the most part, these two boys had been left out of the history, the narrative of that day. Once I found out about them, I knew that whatever work I made would have to include their presence.

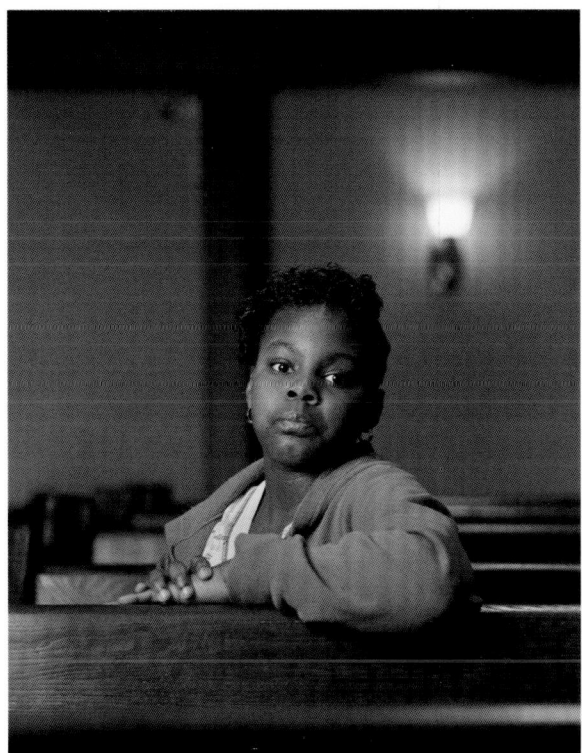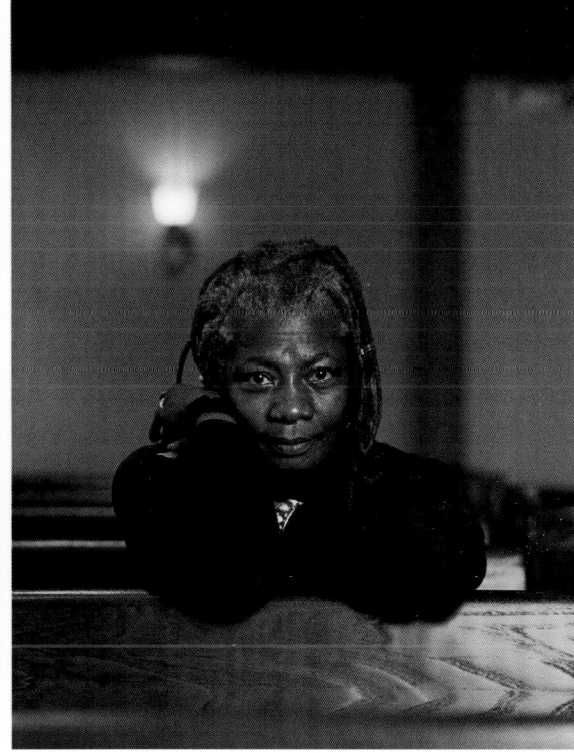

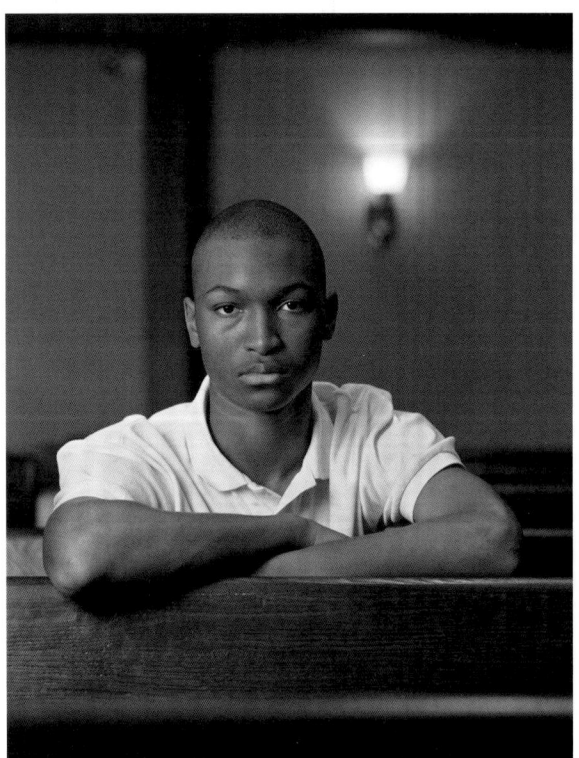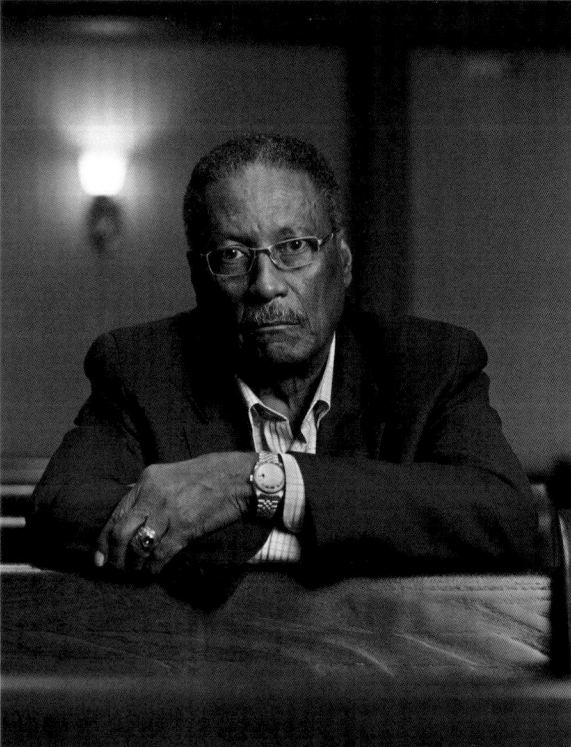

How do you bring what happened fifty years ago into the present in a palpable way? How do you collapse the past and the present?

I grappled with what I could make in response to this horrible history, both conceptually and materially. After six years of visiting Birmingham, I ultimately decided to make portraits of African American children who were the same ages as the six who were killed in 1963. Three of the girls were fourteen and one was eleven; the boys were thirteen and sixteen.

Though the bombing was well known, the four girls were referred to collectively in the history rather than as individualized people—they were almost an abstraction. I wanted to give them a tangible presence through the lives of young people now. And then, to further mark what was lost, I photographed African American adults who were the ages the six young people would have been if they had lived. In order to visualize the passage of fifty years since the bombing, I paired the photographs into diptychs: the portrait of the eleven-year-old girl was with the portrait of a sixty-one-year-old woman, the sixteen-year-old boy with a sixty-six-year-old man.

Dawoud Bey
Michael-Anthony Allen and George Washington,
Birmingham, Alabama, 2012

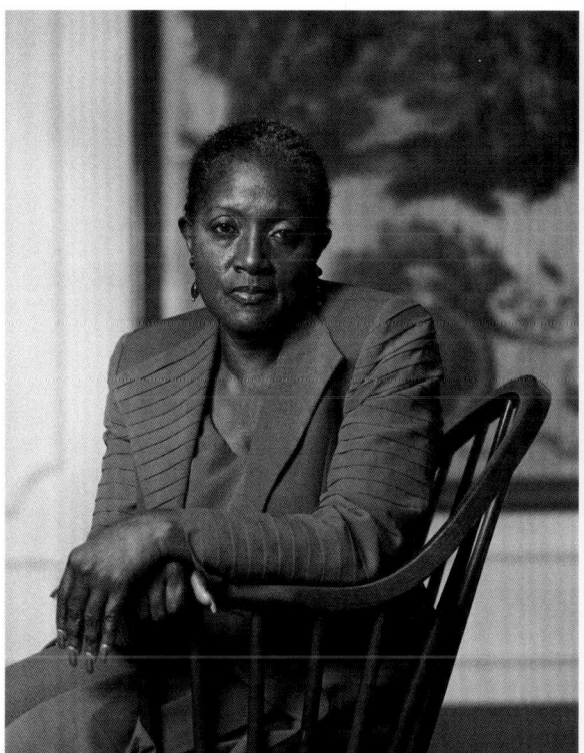 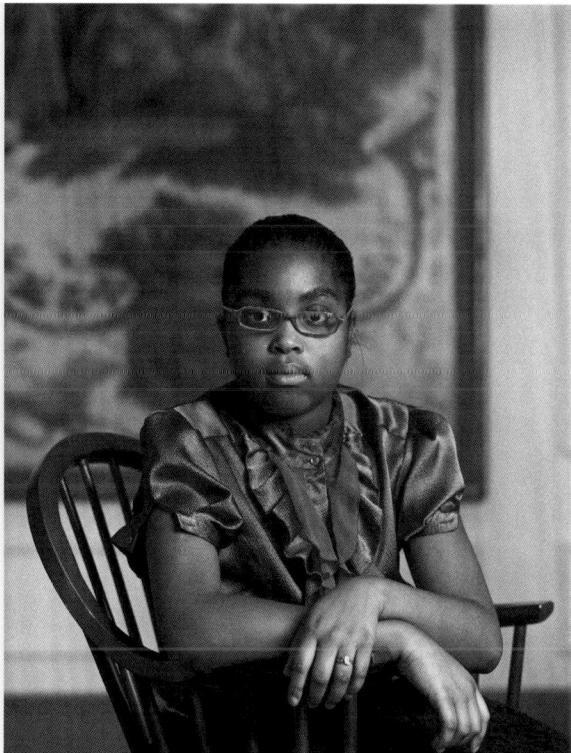

I wanted to make the work in places that were part of the social history of 1963. I chose Reverend Fred Shuttlesworth's church, the Bethel Baptist Church, as one of the locations. I thought it was important that I make photographs there because that church had played a central role in the civil rights movement. I had a meeting with the current minister who understood what I was trying to do and made the sanctuary, which had just undergone a historical restoration, available to me.

I chose the second location, the Birmingham Museum of Art, because in the 1960s the museum, like all public institutions in the South, had been segregated until they implemented a "negro day" one day a week. I wanted to photograph African Americans at the museum—a place that had restricted their access in the past—knowing the pictures would also be shown there. I wanted both parts of this social history to surround the subjects: the black communal space of the church and the more problematic segregated space of the museum.

Dawoud Bey
Betty Salvage and Faith Speights,
Birmingham, Alabama, 2012

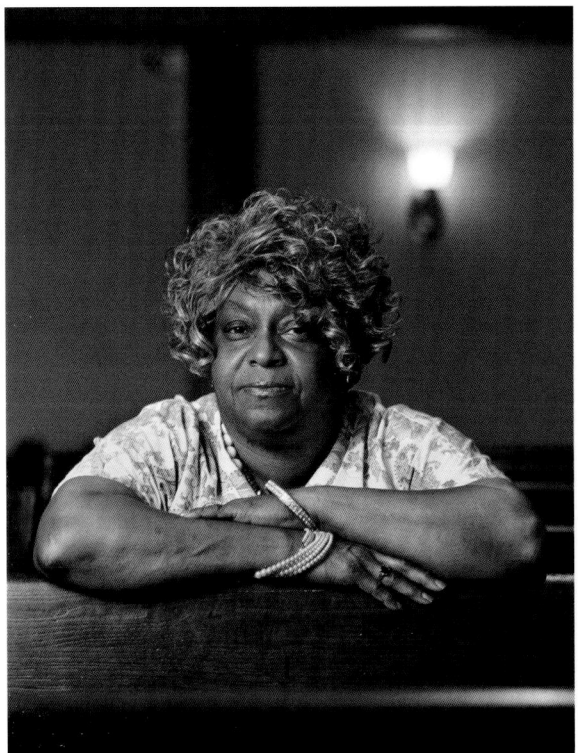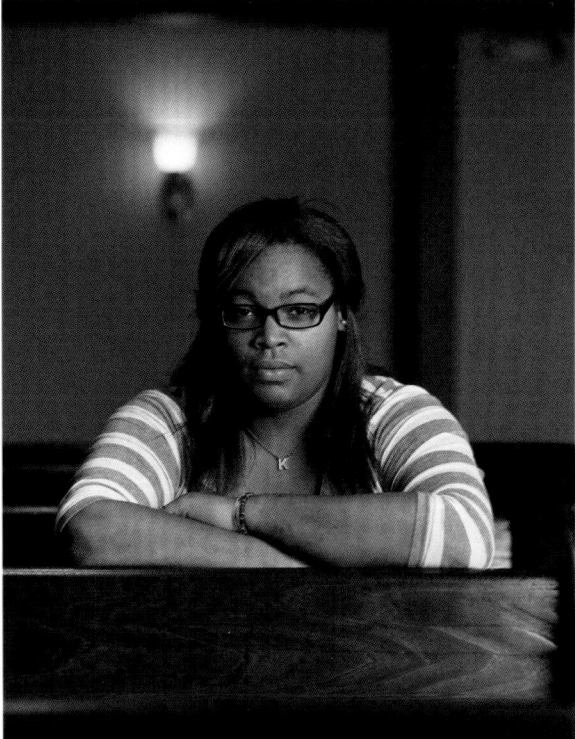

I had approached the museum during one of my visits to ask if they would be interested in commissioning this work, and they were. Once I had the deadline of an
exhibition date, I spent about six months in Birmingham, putting out calls on every
possible platform to cast the subjects—listings on Craigslist and social media,
flyers in beauty parlors and barbershops, social service agencies, and greasy-spoon
restaurants. As I wasn't just photographing young folks and older folks—they
had to be very specific ages—the outreach had to be deep and continuous.

    The diptychs were composed of two portraits made separately and brought
together later. Not every portrait I made of an eleven-year-old girl could be
paired with every portrait of a sixty-one-year-old woman. In order to make strong
diptychs, I had to photograph a lot people. Nights, weekends, whenever people
were available, I went to the museum and to the church. I photographed pretty
much every day over the course of those six months.

    When I made the diptychs, I was looking for ways in which the young person
and the older person seemed to relate to each other in order to create something
coherent out of two separate portraits. These points of continuity make each
portrait resonate more powerfully.

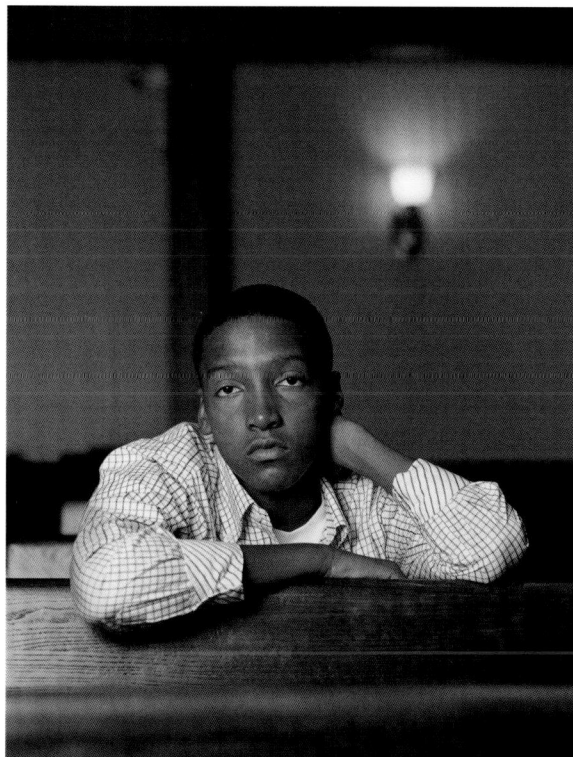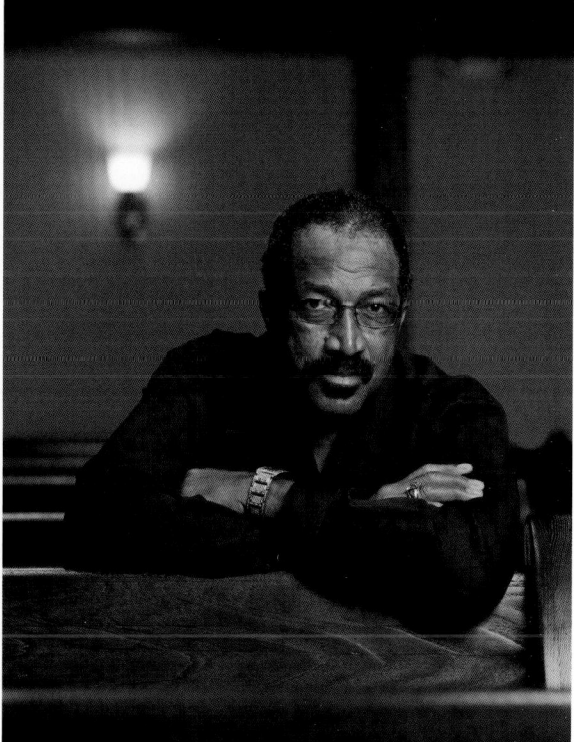

I made instant prints as I went along, so I had a record of each portrait. When a young girl walked in, I would see if she might pair well with the women I had photographed and then place her on the right or left accordingly. If I didn't spot a match, I would randomly decide—I was constantly putting together this puzzle. Some just never found a partner because they didn't work with others. And with portraits, you can't just flop them; it always looks off. I ended up with thirty-two portraits, sixteen pairs, that worked together.

From the beginning, I chose to make black-and-white photographs because of the material's photographic history; it implies the past. But I also chose to print the diptychs rather large: they are contemporary in scale but allude to the historical nature of the project.

Dawoud Bey
Braxton McKinney and Lavon Thomas,
Birmingham, Alabama, 2012

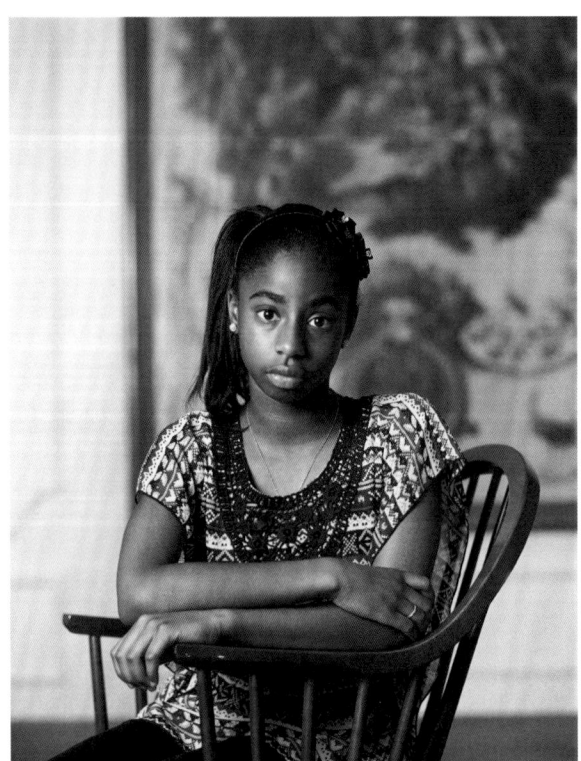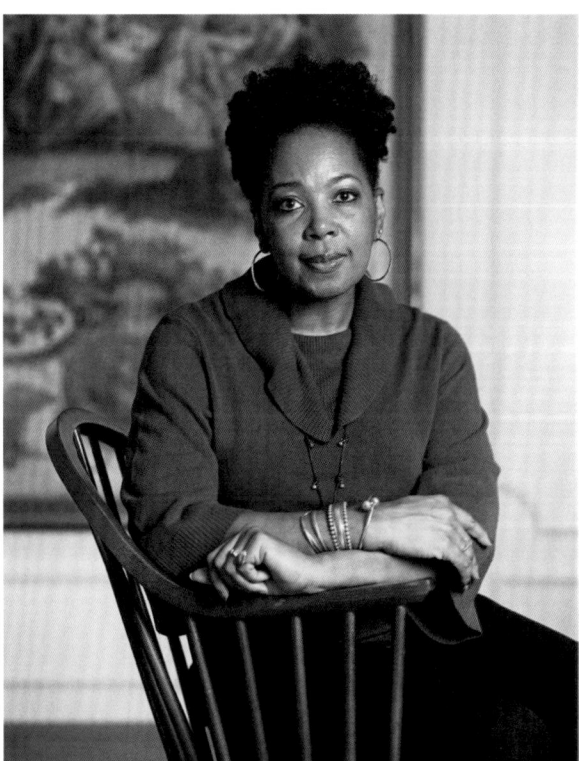

It Could Have Been Her

Any time I photograph someone, they're in a particular context that we both understand and they bring themselves to the situation. In this case, each person was being photographed to bear witness to history. They're bringing that with them to the picture as well. They're not just there to have a portrait made; they're there to be photographed in this place by an artist making work about the church bombing. That's the context.

The adults I photographed were in their sixties and all remembered that day, of course, because they were in Birmingham—some of them heard the bomb going off, some of them knew the girls who had been killed. They were living embodiments of the memory of that morning.

It was extremely important that each portrait present fully a fleshed out person. For me, each girl could have been, and at that moment *was*, one of the girls in the 16th Street Baptist Church. It's one thing to say, "Four little girls were killed in the bombing of the church." They're faceless entities. But when you see the girl in the portrait, you realize that with a change in historical circumstance, it could have been her. This is what an eleven-year-old girl looks like; imagine this girl in front of you being struck by the force of the blast that blew Denise McNair's head off of her shoulders. You think about that when you look at the picture.

Making the pictures was a deeply moving and difficult experience. Each time a young girl came in to be photographed, my heart would catch because that's what these girls looked like. That's who they were. They were not just "four little girls."

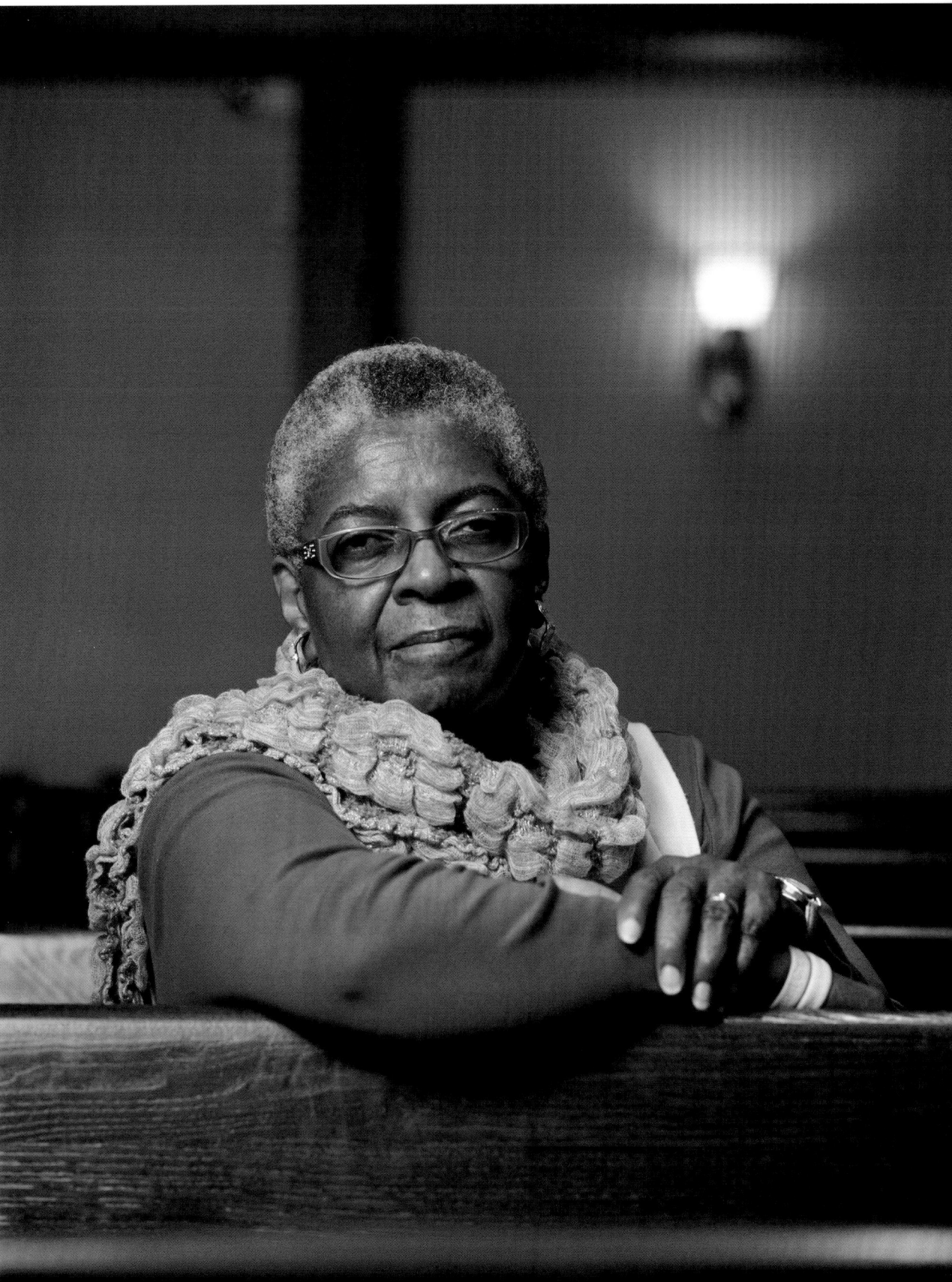

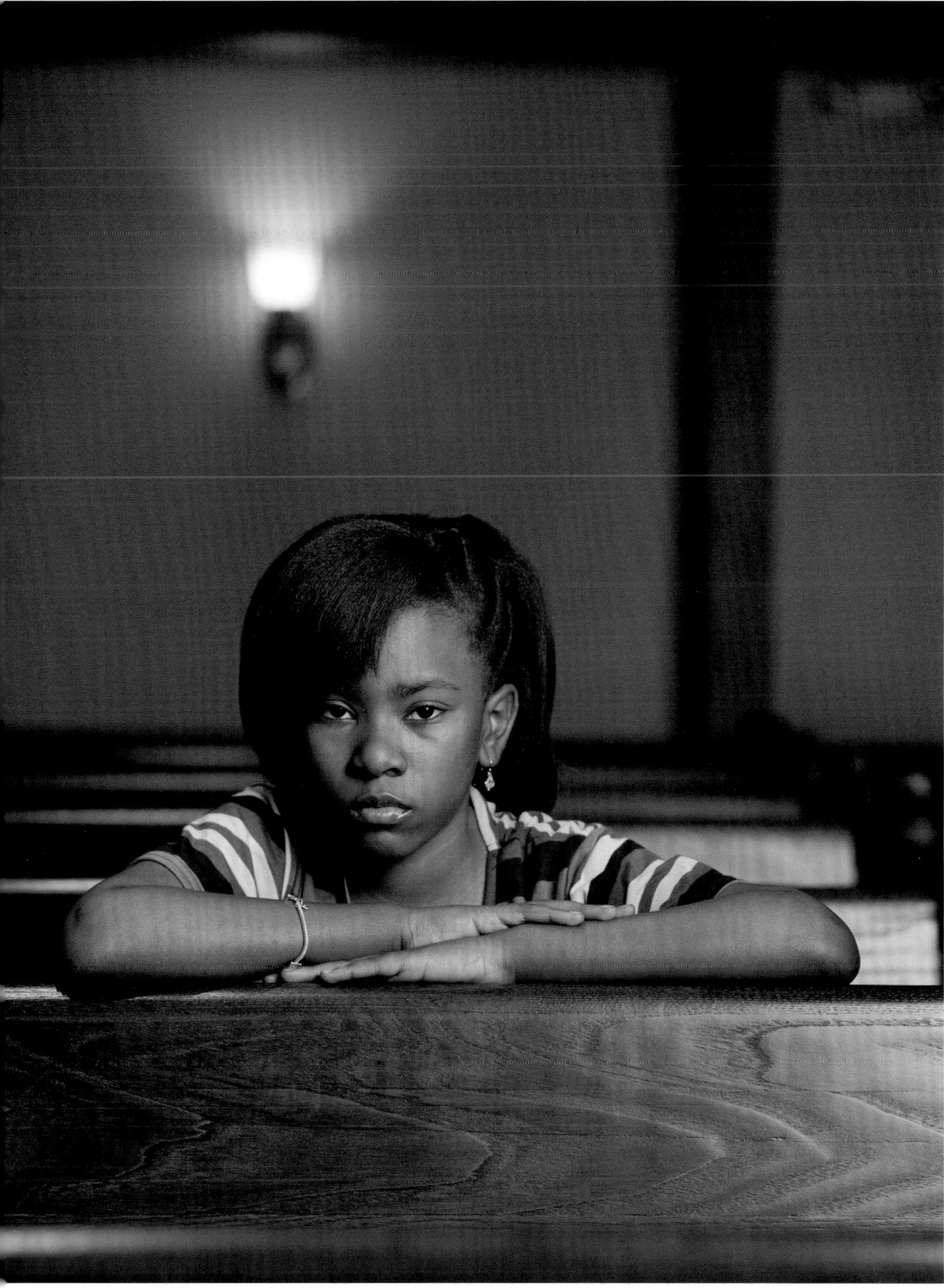

The Idea in Front of You

All of these efforts took a lot of relationship building. Many people, particularly the men, were reluctant to participate because it was a traumatic history. The older subjects grew up in a segregated time—it didn't mean anything to them that I was working with the museum. In fact, later when I told them to come to the museum, some went to the Birmingham Civil Rights Institute instead. It was obvious that this was the first time many of the adults had ever been to that museum. When I met Carolyn Maul McKinstry, who was there the day of the bombing, she reached out more deeply into the community than I or the museum could. It was Carolyn telling the men, "You can do this," that brought them forward.

If no older men had come forward, then there would have been no project, or the project would have been very odd conceptually. There was always this huge, looming potential for failure as I was doing the work. And that's something every artist knows. When you're working, you face a kind of wall, but you also have this idea in front of you and you keep pushing ahead hoping that it happens. I just knew that this project had to happen. And I had to do all that I could to make it happen by simply continuing to work.

Pages 114–15
Dawoud Bey
Mary Parker and Caela Cowan,
Birmingham, Alabama, 2012

Right
Dawoud Bey
Fred Stewart II and Tyler Collins,
Birmingham, Alabama, 2012

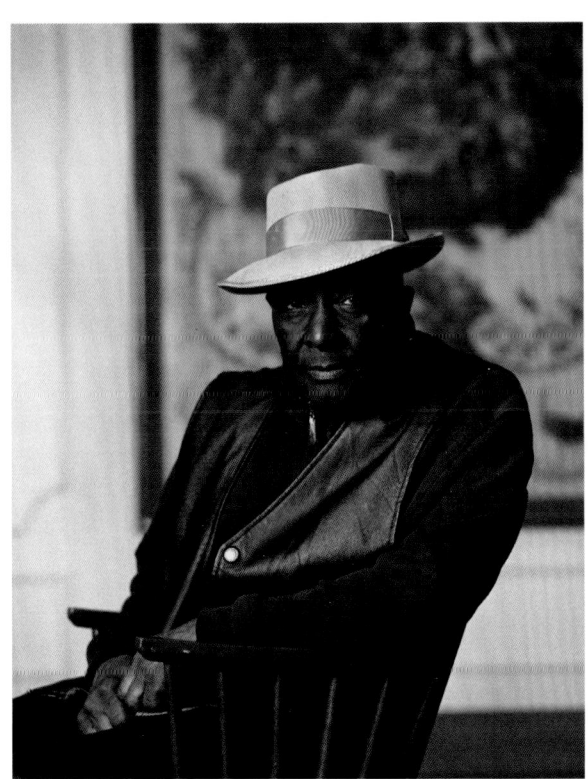
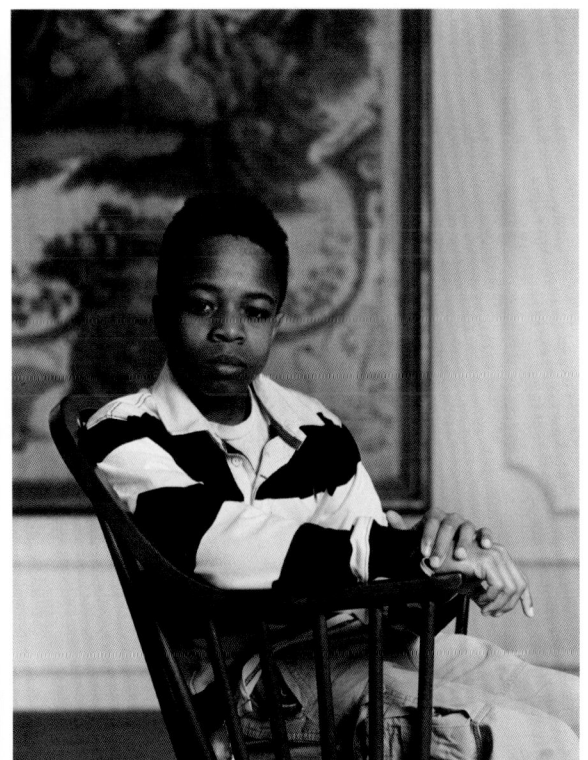

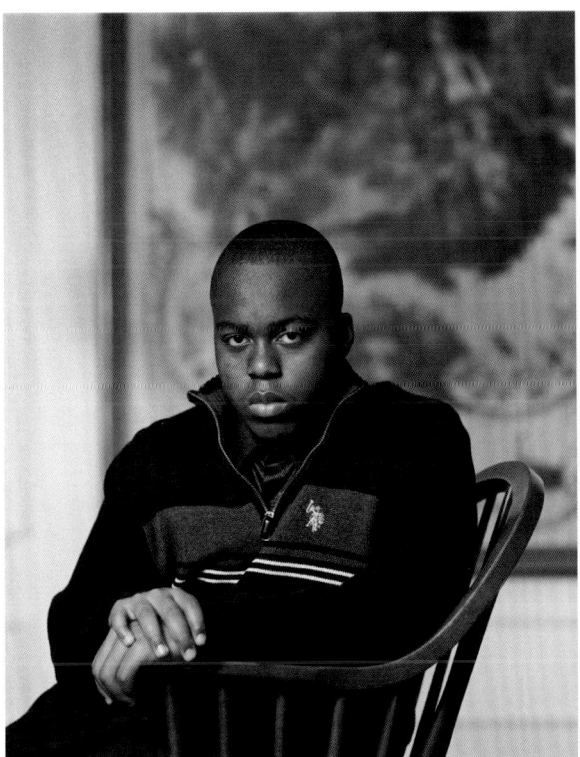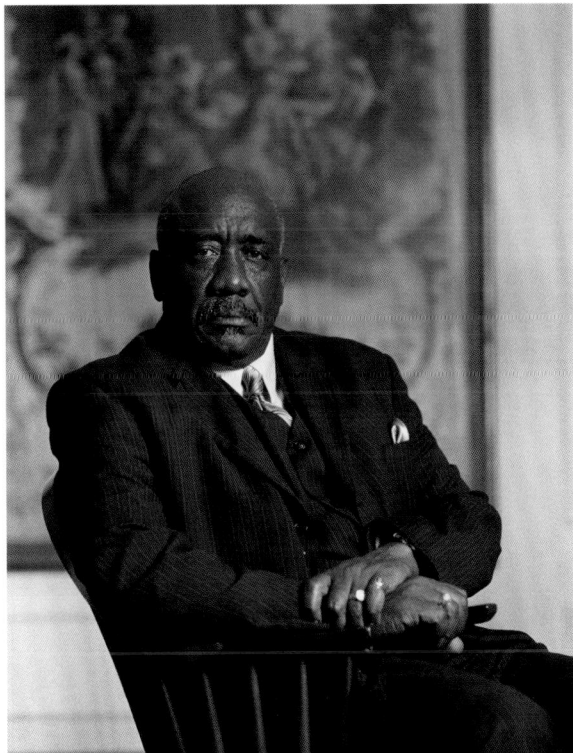

Everything I allude to in these pictures, I think, is a result of learning and living with the history. It took six years before I felt I had a deep enough understanding to make photographs or had the right to. I have to believe that all of my experiences—researching, getting to know people, and building community—during those years of going back and forth, made their way into the work in some way.

Photography is how I make my thinking visible and present in the world. There are people, issues, and history that I care about. Part of the motivation for the work is to bring the things that I need to see into the world with the understanding that if it is important enough to me, it will have meaning for someone else as well.

An Act of Faith

The great novelist John Oliver Killens gave me this advice thirty years ago, and it's true: your work should be something that you would be doing regardless of whether the larger market ever responds or not. Making art has to be your own particular obsession. "You have to be a long distance runner," he would say to me and the other young artists and writers who were gathered around him. Be prepared to make work for the long haul.

Making art has never been the safest or easiest pursuit. There is no quick or clever hustle that will sustain you, no one you can meet whose connections will allow you to skip the long hours it takes to produce something of substance. Every photographer is faced with creative challenges, as well as the realities of having to somehow maintain a practice during times of economic uncertainty. Making art is an act of faith.

To make it over the long haul, I encourage you to create a community of support with other photographers and artists. Contrary to what some might think, no one gets there, wherever "there" is, on their own—there is no lone genius out there making breakthroughs without a supportive and sometimes challenging community of peers. Those ongoing critical conversations will sharpen your thinking about and your ambition for the work.

Some of the opportunities you seek will come out of your community, and others you will to have to create, not only for yourself but indeed for others. So much of my career has been made possible through relationships spanning many years, relationships in which I applauded the work of others as they applauded mine. And it can be this way for you as well. Take the opportunity to encourage one another. Embrace it. There is room for more than one person at the table of opportunity.

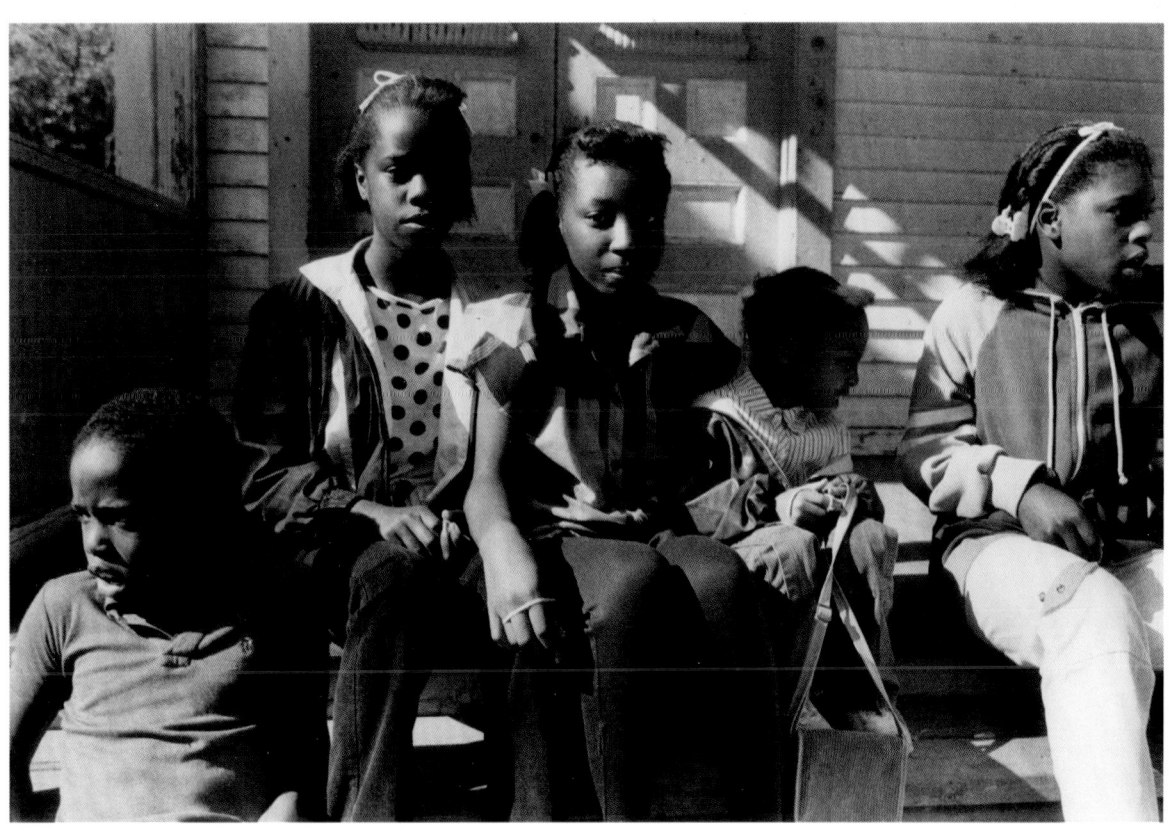

Dawoud Bey
Five Children, Syracuse,
New York, 1985

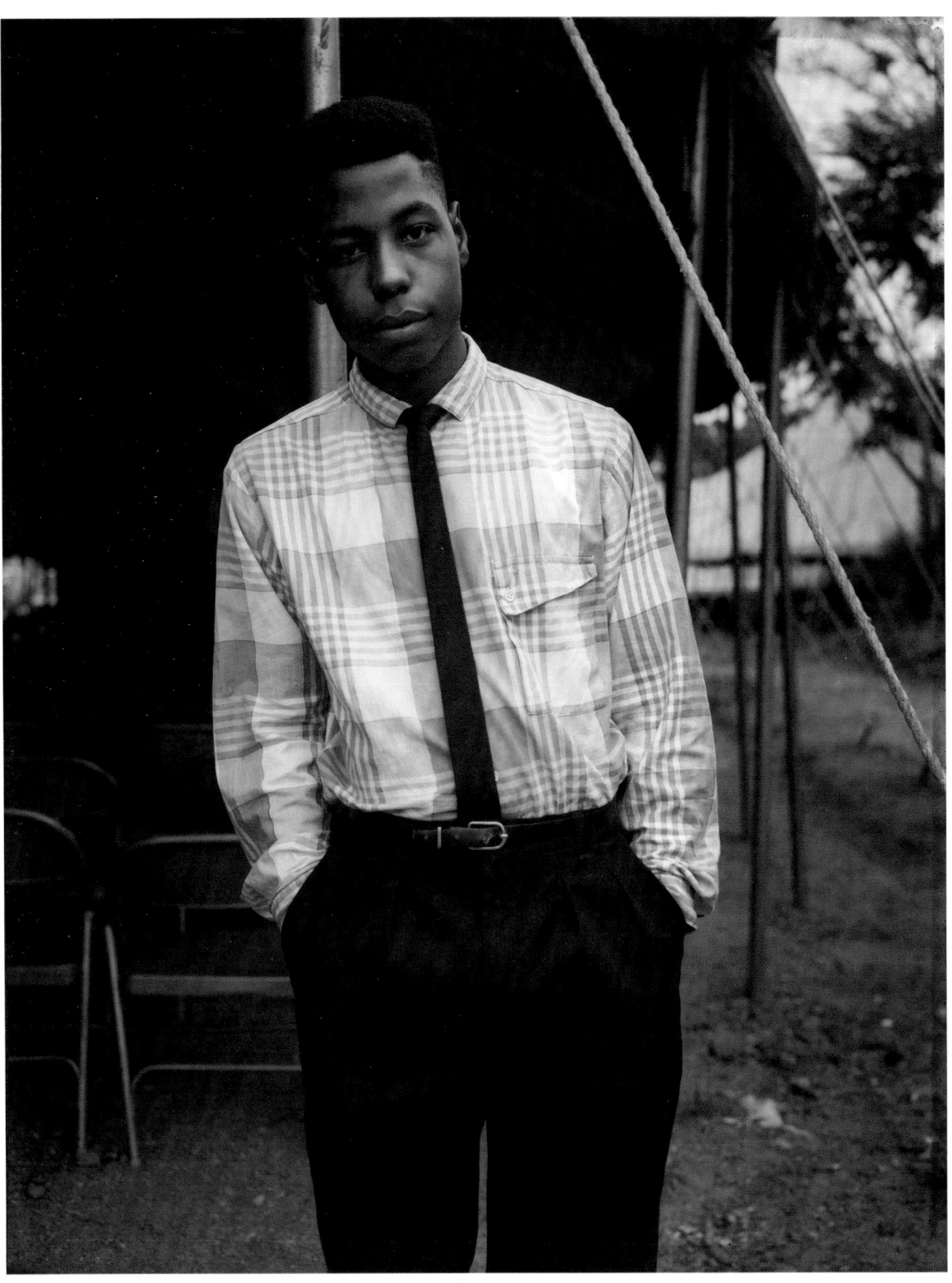

Dawoud Bey
A Young Man at a Tent Revival,
Brooklyn, 1989

The most important thing is to make work that matters, to bring things into the world that have consequence.

For the past twenty-two years, I've taught photography at Columbia College Chicago, where we have a credo to "author the culture of our times." That is something that I believe in deeply, and it's something I encourage everyone who picks up the camera seriously to buy into. Consider how through your own work, your writing, your research, exhibitions you curate, and people you mentor, how you are authoring the culture of these times.

This doesn't dictate the form, or the materials, or the subject matter; just make work that you believe matters and that has the capacity to transform the viewer, and by extension, the larger social community. Having seen your work, viewers have the potential to go back out into the world with new information, and new perceptions—a transformed worldview. This may sound like an overly ambitious agenda, but it is the *only* agenda.

In order to do this, you need to learn how to give your conviction some resonate form, because a sloppy object, a subpar photograph or print, even if well intentioned, is pretty much meaningless. You have to hone your craft and be fluent in the history of the medium, genre, and material to make work that will reach viewers so that the thing you care about becomes something that they care about.

This doesn't happen because you have a good heart; it happens through the quality of the object you make. You need to know how to skillfully and consistently make work. Get an education, whether from a good art or photography program or from obsessively seeking out knowledge on your own. Look at a lot of work, and look at it on the wall, a place that you can see the actual photographs. It's important to see what a well-made photograph looks like. Having a good heart is the place to start, but you have to be able to turn that into pictures that hold the conversation when you're not there, into work that carries your intentions out into the world for you.

While it's not easy, I think that there is also joy in struggle. There is tremendous joy in being a photographer. It's a privilege to determine the way you're going to live and to do the things that you believe matter. Keep the faith!

Recommended Reading/Looking

I've selected this list of books by various photographers who have engaged with the idea of representing communities—some as insiders, some as outsiders. Each has given me something meaningful to consider regarding the theme of community, and I hope you will find them as interesting and useful as I have.

— Dawoud Bey

Shelby Lee Adams, *Appalachian Portraits*, 1993

Jules Allen, *Double Up*, 2011

Richard Avedon, *In the American West*, 1985

Keith Calhoun and Chandra McCormick, *Louisiana Medley*, 2018

Vincent Cianni, *We Skate Hardcore: Photographs from Brooklyn's Southside*, 2004

Paul D'Amato, *Here/Still/Now*, 2018

Roy DeCarava and Langston Hughes, *The Sweet Flypaper of Life*, 1955

Jess T. Dugan and Vanessa Fabbre, *To Survive on This Shore: Photographs and Interviews with Transgender and Gender Nonconforming Older Adults*, 2018

Walker Evans and James Agee, *Let Us Now Praise Famous Men: Three Tenant Families*, 1941

Gerard H. Gaskin, *Legendary: Inside the House Ballroom Scene*, 2013

Jim Goldberg, *Rich and Poor*, 1985

Dave Jordano, *Detroit: Unbroken Down*, 2015

Irving Penn, *Small Trades*, 2009

Larry Racioppo, *Brooklyn Before: Photographs, 1971–1983*, 2018

Joseph Rodriguez, *East Side Stories: Gang Life in East LA*, 2000

Milton Rogovin, *Triptychs: Buffalo's Lower West Side Revisited*, 1994

August Sander, *People of the 20th Century*, 2002

Jeffrey Henson Scales, *House*, 2016

THE PHOTOGRAPHY WORKSHOP SERIES

Dawoud Bey

on Photographing People and Communities

Photographs and texts by Dawoud Bey
Introduction by Brian Ulrich

First edition, 2019
Printed in China
10 9 8 7 6 5 4 3

Front cover (clockwise from top left): *A Boy in Front of the Loew's 125th Street Movie Theatre, Harlem*, 1976; *Four Children at Lenox Avenue, Harlem*, 1977; *Kevin, Phillips Academy, Andover, Massachusetts*, 2005; *Hillary and Taro, Chicago*, 1992; *Mgbechi, Phillips Academy, Andover, Massachusetts*, 2005
Back cover (from top): *Odalys, Chadsey High School, Detroit*, 2003; *Two Girls at Lady D's, Harlem*, 1976; *A Woman at Fulton Street and Washington Avenue, Brooklyn*, 1988

Library of Congress Control Number:
2016957036
ISBN 978-1-59711-337-3

Editor: Denise Wolff
Editorial Assistant: Charlotte Chudy
Designer: Ann Griffin, Zürich
Senior Production Manager: True Sims
Production Managers: Nelson Chan, Bryan Krueger
Copy Editor: Alexa Dilworth
Senior Text Editor: Susan Ciccotti
Work Scholars: David Arkin, Bowen Fernie, Charis Morgan

To order Aperture books, or inquire about group or gift orders, contact:
orders@aperture.org

For information about Aperture trade distribution worldwide, visit:
aperture.org/distribution

The staff of the Aperture book program includes:
Sarah Meister, Executive Director; Lesley A. Martin, Editor at Large; Emily Patten, Managing Editor, Books; Caroline Foulke, Assistant to Managing Editor; Iesha E. Coppin-Forde, Editorial Assistant, Books; Senior Text Editor; Isla Ng, Copy Editor/Proofreader; Minjee Cho, Production Director; Andrea Chlad, Production Manager; Thomas Bollier, Production Consultant; Karina Eckmeier, Designer and Project Manager; Kellie McLaughlin, Director of Sales and Marketing; Richard Gregg, Sales Director, Books

aperture

548 West 28th Street, 4th Floor
New York, NY 10001
aperture.org

The Photography Workshop Series is made possible, in part, with generous support from the Besson/Cooper Fund on behalf of Sb Cooper and Rebecca L. Besson.

Aperture is a nonprofit publisher dedicated to creating insight, community, and understanding through photography.

Image Credits: Page 14: © The Richard Avedon Foundation; Page 17: © The Irving Penn Foundation; Page 19: © James Van Der Zee, Courtesy Donna Mussenden Van Der Zee; Page 22: © Bruce Davidson, Courtesy Magnum Photos; Page 104: © Frank Dandridge/The LIFE Images Collection/Getty Images